FRESH DESIGNS
SWEATERS

FEATURING DESIGNS BY

Alexandra Virgiel
Belinda Too
Cheryl Niamath
Gwen Kern
Karen Bourquin
Pamela Wynne
Rosalyn Jung
Sylvia Cannizzaro
Tori Gurbisz
Vera Kaltenecker

AND PHOTOGRAPHY BY

Robert Gladys / Fractured Photography

COOPERATIVE PRESS
Cleveland, OH
cooperativepress.com

FRESH DESIGNS: SWEATERS

Library of Congress Control Number: 2012936576
ISBN 13: 978-1-937513-05-4
First Edition
Published by Cooperative Press
http://www.cooperativepress.com

Patterns © 2012, their designers, as credited
Photos © 2012, Robert Gladys, Fractured Photography (fracturedphotography.com)

Makeup by Elle Gemma
Models: Terra Incognita, Arabella Proffer, Susan Prahst

Every effort has been made to ensure that all the information in this book is accurate at the time of publication, however Cooperative Press neither endorses nor guarantees the content of external links referenced in this book.

If you have questions or comments about this book, or need information about licensing, custom editions, special sales, or academic/corporate purchases, please contact Cooperative Press: info@cooperativepress.com or 13000 Athens Ave C288, Lakewood, OH 44107 USA

No part of this book may be reproduced in any form, except brief excerpts for the purpose of review, without prior written permission of the publisher. Thank you for respecting our copyright.

FOR COOPERATIVE PRESS

Senior Editor: Shannon Okey
Assistant Editor: Elizabeth Green Musselman
Developmental Editor: Abra Forman
Technical Editor: Alexandra Virgiel, with additional editing by Jaya Purswani
Production Manager: MJ Kim
With additional assistance by Sarah Jo Burch

TABLE OF CONTENTS

ALEXANDRA VIRGIEL — Claire M — (page 5)

BELINDA TOO — Lacy Summer Camisole — (page 11)

CHERYL NIAMATH — Anina — (page 15)

GWEN KERN — Beach Vines Pullover — (page 19)

KAREN BOURQUIN — Classic Cabled Crew — (page 23)

PAMELA WYNNE — Ziggy — (page 27)

ROSALYN JUNG — Knots and Cables Vest — (page 33)

SYLVIA CANNIZZARO — Sophia Goes to Houdan — (page 41)

TORI GURBISZ — Everything Nice Hoodie — (page 47)

VERA KALTENECKER — Crescent — (page 53)

ACKNOWLEDGMENTS — (page 57)
ABOUT COOPERATIVE PRESS AND THE FRESH DESIGNS SERIES — (page 58)

CLAIRE M
BY ALEXANDRA VIRGIEL

EXPERIENCED

Short sleeved dolman wrap sweater with extra-long ties, inspired by the wrap-and-tie designs of Claire McCardell.

SIZE
S [M, L, 1X]
Shown in size S.

FINISHED MEASUREMENTS
Chest: 34 [38, 42, 46]"/86.5 [95, 106.5, 117]cm
Length: 22 [23.5, 24.5, 25.75]"/56 [59, 62, 65]cm

MATERIALS
Spirit Trail Fiberworks Birte [75% superwash merino wool, 15% cashmere, 10% bombyx silk; 275yd/251m per 100g skein]; color Rosewood; 4 [5, 5, 5] skeins

24"/60cm US #6/4mm circular needle
Two US#6/4mm dpns, for working i-cord

Removable marker or safety pin

GAUGE
20 sts/29 rows = 4"/10cm in stockinette

STITCH INSTRUCTIONS
RLI (right lifted increase): Use the right needle to pick up the stitch below the next stitch on the left needle. Place it on the left needle, then knit into it. 1 st inc'd.

LLI (left lifted increase): Use the left needle to pick up the back of the stitch 2 below stitch just knitted, then knit into it. 1 st inc'd.

W&t (wrap and turn)
On a RS row: Sl next st pwise wyib, bring yarn to front between needles, return slipped st to LH needle, turn work.

On a WS row: Sl next st pwise wyif, bring yarn to back between needles, return slipped st to LH needle, turn work.

I-cord
With dpn, CO 3 sts. Knit 1 row. *Do not turn work. Draw yarn firmly across back of work and knit row again. Rep from * to desired length.

PATTERN NOTES
This sweater is knit in three pieces: left back and front, center back, and right back and front. Left and right are begun at the bottom back edge and worked up and over the shoulder to the bottom front edge. Center back is a strip of ribbing that extends from the bottom to the neck edge of the back.

Ribbed neck edging is knit simultaneously with the body of the sweater.

Row gauge is important. If your row gauge is off, the sweater may come out longer or shorter than planned.

PATTERN
LEFT HALF
CO 40 [44, 50, 54] sts.
Row 1 [WS]: *K1, p1; rep from * to end.
Rep last row 5 times more.

Shape waist
Next row [WS]: Purl, inc 0 [1, 0, 1] st in center of row. 40 [45, 50, 55] sts.
Cont in stockinette, work 6 [8, 10, 12] rows even.
Waist dec row [RS]: Knit to last 3 sts, k2tog, k1. 1 st dec'd.
Rep Waist Dec Row on every 14th row twice more. 37 [42, 47, 52] sts.
Work 11 rows even.
Waist inc row [RS]: Knit to last st, m1, k1. 1 st inc'd.
Rep Waist Inc Row on every 14th row twice more. 40 [45, 50, 55] sts.

Work 11 [13, 15, 17] rows even. Piece should measure approx. 12.75

[13.5, 14, 14.5]"/31.5 [33.5, 35, 36]cm from CO edge.

Shape underarm gusset
Gusset inc row [RS]: Knit to last st, m1, k1. 1 st inc'd.
Rep Gusset Inc Row on every RS row 6 times more. 47 [52, 57, 62] sts.

Shape sleeve
Use cable method to cast on 9 sts at beg of next row [WS], purl to end of row. 56 [61, 66, 71] sts.
Work 46 [50, 54, 60] rows even. Sleeve should measure approx. 6.5 [7, 7.5, 8.5]"/16 [17.5, 19, 21]cm from CO edge.

Shape back shoulder and neck
Row 1 [RS]: [K1, p1] 9 [10, 11, 12] times, knit to last 8 [9, 10, 10] sts, w&t.
Row 2 [WS]: Purl to last 18 [20, 22, 24] sts, [k1, p1] 9 [10, 11, 12] times.
Row 3: Rib 18 [20, 22, 24] sts, knit to 8 [9, 10, 10] sts before last wrapped st, w&t.
Row 4: Purl to last 18 [20, 22, 24] sts, rib to end.
Rows 5-6: Rep Rows 3-4.
Row 7: BO 12 [14, 16, 18] sts, rib 6 sts, knit to 8 [9, 10, 10] sts before last wrapped st, w&t.
Row 8: Purl to last 6 sts, rib to end.
Row 9 [RS]: Rib 6, knit to end, picking up and knitting wraps tog with wrapped sts.

You are now at the top of the shoulder/middle of the sleeve. Place a marker in the fabric at the end of the last row. 44 [47, 50, 53] sts.

Shape front shoulder
Row 1 and all WS rows: Purl to last 6 sts, rib 6.
Row 2 [RS]: Rib 6, k6 [5, 4, 7], w&t.
Row 4: Rib 6, knit to last wrapped st, pick up and knit wrap tog with wrapped st, k7 [8, 9, 9], w&t.
Rows 6 and 8: Rep Row 4.
Row 10: Rib 6, knit to end, picking up and knitting last wrap tog with wrapped st.
Work even, keeping 6 sts at neck edge in rib, for 15 [15, 15, 17] rows.

Shape front neck
Front neck inc row [RS]: Rib 6, k1, LLI, knit to end. 1 st inc'd.
Rep Front Neck Inc Row on every RS row 44 [47, 50, 53] times more, for a total of 45 [48, 51, 54] sts inc'd at neck edge.

AT THE SAME TIME, continue to shape sleeve, gusset and waist as foll.

Shape sleeve
Work even until sleeve from marker is 46 [50, 54, 60] rows long (counted at outside edge, not over the short row shaping).
Next row [WS]: BO 9 sts, work to end.
Gusset dec row [RS]: Work to last 3 sts, k2tog, k1. 1 st dec'd.
Rep Gusset Dec Row on every RS row 6 times more. 7 sts dec'd.

Shape waist
Work 11 [13, 15, 17] rows even.
Waist dec row [RS]: Work to last 3 sts, k2tog, k1. 1 st dec'd.
Rep Waist Dec Row on every 14th row twice more.
Work 11 rows even. Note: The final Front Neck Inc Row should fall on Row 6 of these 11 rows. After neck incs are complete, work straight at that edge, keeping first 6 sts in rib.
Waist inc row [RS]: Work to last st, m1, k1. 1 st inc'd.
Rep Waist Inc Row on every 14th row twice more.
After all shaping is complete, there should be 73 [79, 85, 91] sts.
Work 7 [9, 11, 13] rows even.
Next row [RS]: *K1, p1; rep from * to last st, k1.
Work in k1, p1 rib for 5 more rows. BO all sts.

RIGHT HALF
CO 40 [44, 50, 54] sts.
Row 1 [WS]: *P1, k1; rep from * to end.
Rep last row 5 times more.

Shape waist
Next row [WS]: Purl, inc 0 [1, 0, 1] st in center of row. 40 [45, 50, 55] sts.
Cont in stockinette, work 6 [8, 10, 12] rows even.
Waist dec row [RS]: K1, ssk, knit to end. 1 st dec'd.
Rep Waist Dec Row on every 14th row twice more. 37 [42, 47, 52] sts.
Work 11 rows even.
Waist inc row [RS]: K1, m1, knit to end. 1 st inc'd.
Rep Waist Inc Row on every 14th row twice more. 40 [45, 50, 55] sts.
Work 11 [13, 15, 17] rows even. Piece should measure approx. 12.75 [13.5, 14, 14.5]"/31.5 [33.5, 35, 36]cm from CO edge.

Shape underarm gusset
Gusset inc row [RS]: K1, m1, knit to end. 1 st inc'd.
Rep Gusset Inc Row on every RS row 6 times more. 47 [52, 57, 62] sts.
Work 1 WS row even.

Shape sleeve

(continues page 8)

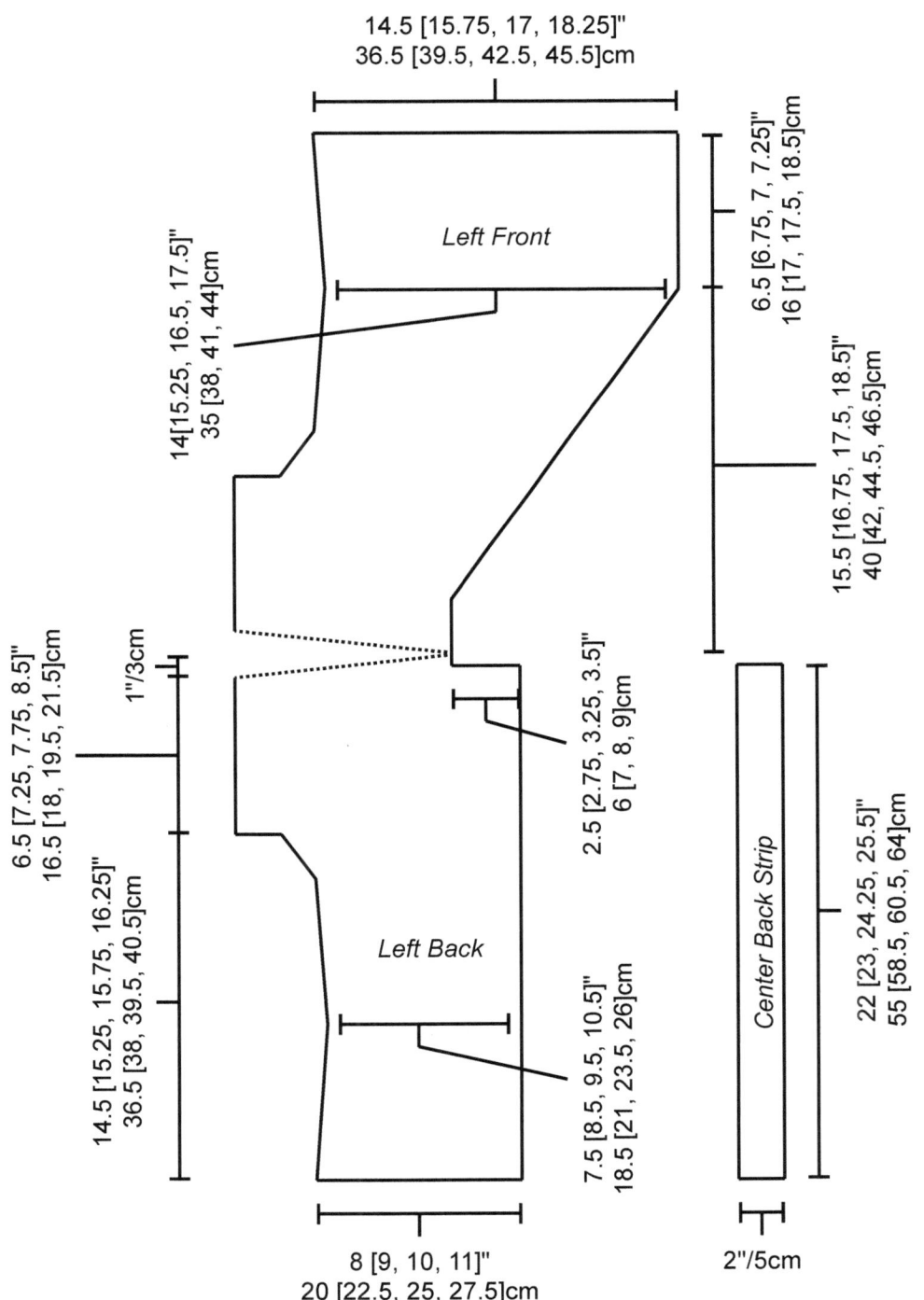

Use cable method to CO 9 sts at beg of next row [RS], knit to end of row. 56 [61, 66, 71] sts.
Work 46 [50, 54, 60] rows even. Sleeve should measure approx. 6.5 [7, 7.5, 8.5]"/16 [17.5, 19, 21]cm from CO edge.

Shape back shoulder and neck
Row 1 [WS]: [P1, k1] 9 [10, 11, 12] times, purl to last 8 [9, 10, 10] sts, w&t.
Row 2 [RS]: Knit to last 18 [20, 22, 24] sts, [p1, k1] 9 [10, 11, 12] times.
Row 3: Rib 18 [20, 22, 24] sts, purl to 8 [9, 10, 10] sts before last wrapped st, w&t.
Row 4: Knit to last 18 [20, 22, 24] sts, rib to end.
Rows 5-6: Rep Rows 3-4.
Row 7: BO 12 [14, 16, 18] sts, rib 6 sts, purl to 8 [9, 10, 10] sts before last wrapped st, w&t.
Row 8: Purl to last 6 sts, rib to end.
Row 9 [WS]: Rib 6, purl to end, picking up and purling wraps tog with wrapped sts.

You are now at the top of the shoulder/middle of the sleeve. Pm at end of last row. 44 [47, 50, 53] sts.

Shape front shoulder
Row 1 and all RS rows: Knit to last 6 sts, rib 6.
Row 2 [WS]: Rib 6, p6 [5, 4, 7], w&t.
Row 4: Rib 6, purl to last wrapped st, pick up and purl wrap tog with wrapped st, k7 [8, 9, 9], w&t.
Rows 6 and 8: Rep Row 4.
Row 10: Rib 6, purl to end, picking up and purling last wrap tog with wrapped st.
Work even, keeping 6 sts at neck edge in rib, for 16 [16, 16, 18] rows.

Shape front neck
Front neck inc row [RS]: Knit to last 7 sts, RLI, k1, rib 6. 1 st inc'd.
Rep Front Neck Inc Row on every RS row 44 [47, 50, 53] times more, for a total of 45 [48, 51, 54] sts inc'd at neck edge.

AT THE SAME TIME, continue to shape sleeve, gusset and waist as foll.

Shape sleeve
Work even until sleeve from marker is 46 [50, 54, 60] rows long (counted at outside edge, not over the short row shaping).
Next row [RS]: BO 9 sts, work to end.
Work 1 WS row even.
Gusset dec row [RS]: K1, ssk, work to end. 1 st dec'd.
Rep Gusset Dec Row on every RS row 6 times more. 7 sts dec'd.

Shape waist
Work 11 [13, 15, 17] rows even.

Waist dec row [RS]: K1, ssk, work to end. 1 st dec'd.
Rep Waist Dec Row on every 14th row twice more.
Work 11 rows even. Note: The final Front Neck Inc Row should fall on Row 6 of these 11 rows. After neck incs are complete, work straight at that edge, keeping last 6 sts in rib.
Waist inc row [RS]: K1, m1, work to end. 1 st inc'd.
Rep Waist Inc Row on every 14th row twice more.
Work 7 [9, 11, 13] rows even. After all shaping is complete, there should be 73 [79, 85, 91] sts.
Next row [RS]: *K1, p1; rep from * to last st, k1.
Work in k1, p1 rib for 5 more rows. BO all sts.

CENTER BACK STRIP
CO 15 sts. Work k1, p1 rib for 159 [167, 175, 185] rows. BO.

FINISHING
Block pieces to schematic measurements.

Sleeve edging
With RS facing, pick up and knit 72 [78, 84, 90] sts across end of sleeve. Work in k1, p1 rib for 6 rows. BO.

Ties (make 2)
Work i-cord for your waist measurement plus 12"/30cm. K3tog and fasten off.

Use mattress stitch to seam left and right halves to center back strip. Sew underarm and side seams, leaving 0.5"/1cm open on either side of waist to thread ties through. Attach ties. Weave in ends.

ABOUT ALEXANDRA VIRGIEL
Alexandra Virgiel is a designer and technical editor. Find her on Ravelry as virgiel.

LACY SUMMER CAMISOLE

BY BELINDA TOO

INTERMEDIATE

A lovely little piece of seamless simplicity, this camisole makes the most of both your curves and your yarn. Worked in a lace pattern that is easily memorized, the camisole is knit from the top down – meaning that you can use every last inch of this gorgeous silk-merino blend. Knitting this garment in the round results in a smooth, seamless fit.

SIZE
XS [S, M, L, 1X, 2X]
Shown in size XS

FINISHED MEASUREMENTS
Chest (unstretched): 20.5 [25.25, 29.75, 34.25, 38.75, 41.25]"/51.5 [63, 74.5, 85.5, 97, 103]cm
Length (not including straps): 16.5 [17.25, 18, 18.75, 19.5, 20.25]"/42 [44, 45.5, 47.5, 49.5, 51.5]cm

The garment is designed to be very close-fitting. Choose a size 6-10"/15-25cm smaller than your actual bust measurement.

MATERIALS
Serenknitty Sublime Sock [50% merino wool, 50% silk; 430yd/400m per 100g skein]; color: Gold Leaf; 1 [2, 2, 2, 3, 3] skeins. (Note Serenknitty is now madcolorfiberarts.com.)

24"/60cm US #4/3.5mm circular needle
US #4/3.5mm straight needles
Spare US #6/4mm needle for binding off

Stitch markers
Tapestry needle

GAUGE
28 sts/37 rows = 4"/10cm in lace patt with smaller needle, unstretched, unblocked. Because of the stretchy nature of the fabric, gauge is not critical.

PATTERN NOTES
Suggested lengths are given in the pattern, but camisole may be worked to any length desired (or until you run out of yarn!).

PATTERN
UPPER FRONT
CO 68 [76, 84, 92, 100, 108] sts.
Row 1 [RS]: Knit.
Row 2 [WS]: Purl.
Row 3: K4, *p1, yo, k2tog tbl, p1, k4; rep from * to end.
Row 4: P4, *k1, p2, k1, p4; rep from * to end.
Row 5: K4, *p1, k2tog, yo, p1, k4; rep from * to end.
Row 6: Rep Row 4.
Rep Rows 3-6 until piece measures approx. 3 [3, 3, 4, 4, 5]"/7.5 [7.5, 7.5, 10, 10, 12.5]cm, ending with Row 5. At the end of this row, pm for side, use the cable method to CO 68 [92, 116, 140, 164, 172] sts, pm and join to work in the round. 136 [168, 200, 232, 264, 280] sts.

BODY
Rnd 1: *K4, p1, k2, p1; rep from * to 4 sts before side marker, k4, sl m, knit to end.
Rnd 2: *K4, p1, yo, k2tog tbl, p1; rep from * to 4 sts before side marker, k4, sl m, knit to end increasing 8 sts evenly spaced. 144 [176, 208, 240, 272, 288] sts.
Rnd 3: *K4, p1, k2, p1; rep from * to end.
Rnd 4: *K4, p1, k2tog, yo, p1; rep from * to end.
Rnd 5: Rep Rnd 3.
Rnd 6: *K4, p1, yo, k2tog tbl, p1; rep from * to end.
Rep Rnds 3-6 until body measures 16.5 [17.25, 18, 18.75, 19.5, 20.25]"/42 [44, 45.5, 47.5, 49.5, 51.5]cm from top front edge, or desired length, or you're nearly out of yarn, ending with Rnd 6. BO loosely in patt using larger needle.

STRAPS
These can be made at any time after the body is well established, using the other end from your ball of yarn.

With RS facing and straight needles, pick up and knit 4 sts from front top corner. Work in stockinette until strap is desired length. Try on the camisole to check the final length. To try on the camisole, slip all stitches onto a long piece of waste yarn.

Graft strap stitches to the CO stitches of the back using Kitchener Stitch. For larger sizes, you may want to make 2 straps on each side.

FINISHING
Weave in ends. Do not block. The camisole is very close-fitting and will stretch fit to your curves.

ABOUT BELINDA TOO
Belinda Too lives in New Zealand with her husband and two young boys, who are growing up thinking knitting is a completely normal activity. Belinda has recently published two books and iPad apps, 'Blendy Knits Socks' and 'Blendy Knits Again,' available at http://www.blendyknits.com. You can find 'Blendy' on Ravelry.

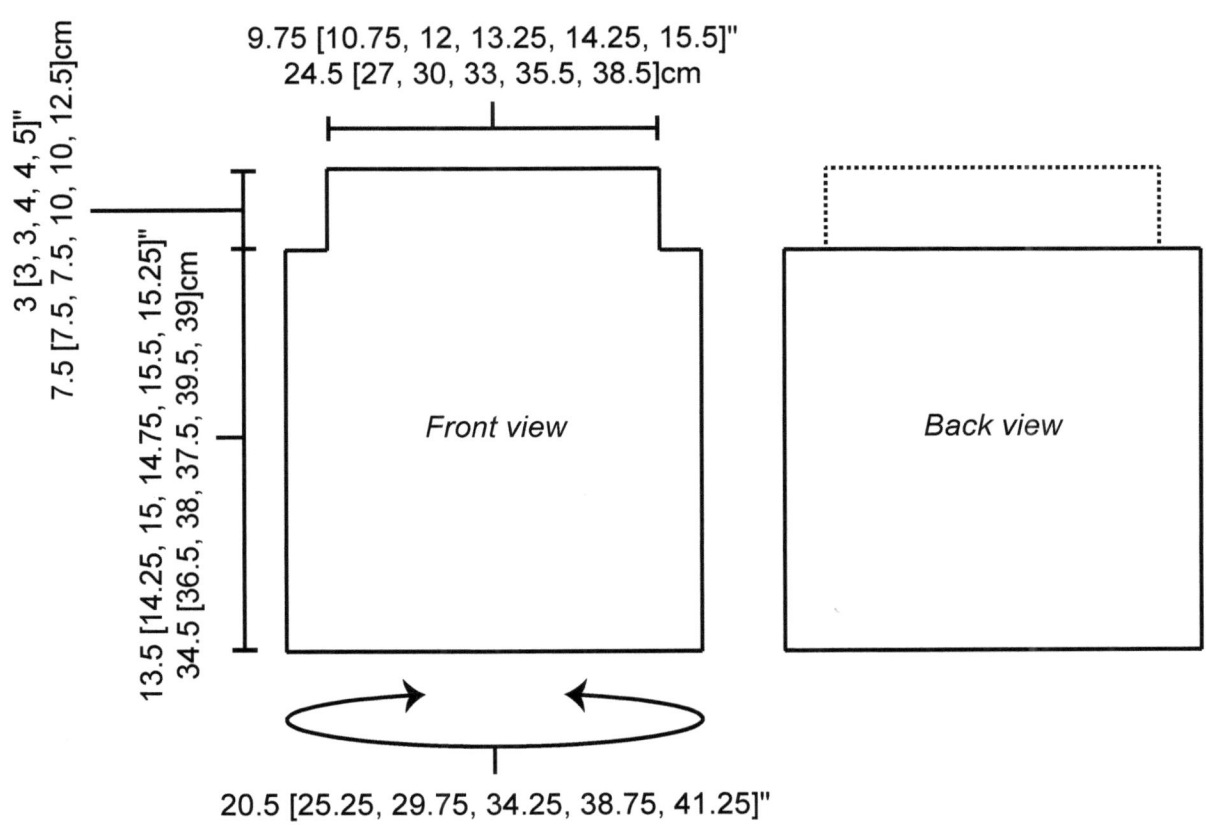

ANINA

BY CHERYL NIAMATH

INTERMEDIATE

Anina is a summery cotton camisole that's perfect paired with a fitted denim skirt or floaty linen trousers. Bare your shoulders and soak up the sun: the adjustable i-cord straps and customizable bust sizing help ensure a perfect fit.

SIZE
XS [S, M, L, XL]
Shown in size M-1

FINISHED MEASUREMENTS
For bust measurements, see chart below.

Length: 14.75 [15.5, 17, 18, 19]"/37.5, 39.5, 43, 45.5, 48.5]cm, not including straps

MATERIALS
Americo Originals Pima Cotton [100% pima cotton, 273yd/250m per 100g skein]; color: J433; 2 (2, 3, 3, 4) skeins

1 24 inch US #7/4.5mm circular needle
1 24-inch US #6/4mm circular needle
Two US #4/3.5mm dpn for working i-cord
Spare US #6/4mm or smaller circular or straight needle

Tapestry needle
Stitch markers
Large safety pin
Stitch holder

GAUGE
22 sts/30 rows = 4"/10cm in 4x1 broken rib with larger needles
22 sts/32 rows = 4"/10cm in seed stitch with smaller needles

STITCH INSTRUCTIONS
4x1 Broken Rib (multiple of 5 sts):
Rnd 1: Knit.
Rnd 2: *K4, p1; rep from * to end.
Rep Rnds 1-2.

Seed Stitch worked in the round (multiple of 2 sts + 1)
Rnd 1: *K1, p1; rep from * to last st, k1.
Rnd 2: *P1, k1; rep from * to last st, p1.
Rep Rnds 1-2.

Seed Stitch worked flat (multiple of 2 sts + 1)
Row 1: *K1, p1; rep from * to last st, k1.
Rep Row 1.

I-cord
With dpn, CO 3 sts. Knit 1 row. *Do not turn work. Draw yarn firmly across back of work and knit row again. Rep from * to desired length.

PATTERN NOTES
Three full bust sizes are provided for each under bust size. Choose the size with a full bust option the closest to your actual bust measurement. If between sizes, choose the smaller.

	Under bust	Full bust 1	Full bust 2	Full bust 3
XS	26.25"/65.5cm	30.25"/76cm	31.5"/78.5cm	32.5"/81.5cm
S	29.75"/74.5cm	34"/85cm	35"/87.5cm	36.25"/90.5
M	33.5"/83.5cm	37.75"/94cm	38.75"/97cm	39.75"/99.5cm
L	36.25"/91cm	40.5"/101.5cm	41.75"/104cm	42.75"/107cm
XL	40"/100cm	44.25"/110.5cm	45.25"/113cm	46.25"/116cm

PATTERN

BODY
With larger circular needle, CO 180 [200, 220, 240, 260] sts using the knitted-on method. Pm and join to work in the round. Place a second marker after 90 [100, 110, 120, 130] sts.
Knit 1 rnd. Purl 1 rnd. Begin working 4x1 broken rib. Work even until body measures 1.5 [1.5, 2, 2, 2.5]"/4 [4, 5, 5, 6.5]cm, ending with Rnd 2 of rib patt.

Shape waist
Dec rnd: *K1, ssk, work to 4 sts before marker, k2tog, k2, sl m; rep from * once more. 4 sts dec'd.
Rep Dec Rnd on every 8th rnd 3 [3, 5, 6, 6] times more, then every 6th rnd 5 [5, 3, 3, 3] times. 144 [164, 184, 200, 220] sts. Work even until body measures 10 [10.5, 11.5, 12, 12.5]"/25.5 [26.5, 29.5, 30.5, 32]cm from CO edge, ending with Rnd 2 of rib patt. Change to smaller needle.

Shape bust
XS-1: K10, m1R, [k4, m1R, k1, m1L] 10 times, k4, m1R, knit to approximate center of back, m1R, knit to end. 167 sts.
XS-2: K4, m1R, k1, m1L, [k4, m1R, k1, m1L] 13 times, knit to approximate center of back, m1R, knit to end. 173 sts.
XS-3: K3, m1, [k2, m1R] 33 times, knit to approximate center of back, m1R, knit to end. 179 sts.

S-1: K15, m1R, [k4, m1R, k1, m1L] 10 times, k4, m1, knit to approximate center of back, m1R, knit to end. 187 sts.
S-2: K9, m1R, k1, m1L, [k4, m1R, k1, m1L] 13 times, knit to approximate center of back, m1R, knit to end. 193 sts.
S-3: K2, m1R, [k3, m1R, k2, m1R] 15 times, k2, m1R, knit to approximate center of back, m1R, knit to end. 199 sts.

M-1: K20, m1R, [k4, m1R, k1, m1L] 10 times, k4, m1R, knit to approximate center of back, m1R, knit to end. 207 sts.
M-2: K14, m1R, k1, m1L, [k4, m1R, k1, m1L] 13 times, knit to approximate center of back, m1R, knit to end. 213 sts.
M-3: K5, m1R, [k4, m1R, k1, m1L] 16 times, k4, m1R, knit to approximate center of back, m1R, knit to end. 219 sts.

L-1: K20, m1R, [k4, m1R, k1, m1L] 10 times, k4, m1R, knit to approximate center of back, m1R, knit to end. 223 sts.
L-2: K19, m1R, k1, m1L, [k4, m1R, k1, m1L] 13 times, knit to approximate center of back, m1R, knit to end. 229 sts.
L-3: K10, m1R, [k4, m1R, k1, m1L] 16 times, k4, m1R, knit to approximate center of back, m1R, knit to end. 235 sts.

XL-1: K25, m1R, [k4, m1R, k1, m1L] 10 times, k4, m1, knit to approximate center of back, m1R, knit to end. 243 sts.
XL-2: K24, m1R, k1, m1L, [k4, m1R, k1, m1L] 13 times, knit to approximate center of back, m1R, knit to end. 249 sts.
XL-3: K10, m1R, [k4, m1R, k1, m1L] 16 times, k4, m1R, knit to approximate center of back, m1R, knit to end. 255 sts.

All sizes:
Knit 1 rnd.
Change to seed st and work 12 [12, 14, 16, 18] rnds even.

UPPER FRONT
Row 1: BO 2 [2, 3, 3, 3] sts, work to marker, turn. Leave back sts on a holder or spare needle.
Row 2 [WS]: BO 2 [2, 3, 3, 3] sts, work to end.
Row 3: Ssk, work to last 2 sts, k2tog. 2 sts dec'd.
Row 4: P1, work in seed st to last st, p1.
Rep Rows 3-4 4 [4, 6, 6, 8] times more.

Current stitch count:
XS: 80/86/92; S: 90/96/102; M: 94/100/106; L: 102/108/114; XL: 108/114/120.

Work even, if necessary, until front measures 1.5 [1.75, 2, 2.25, 2.5]"/3.5 [4.5, 4.5, 5.5, 6]cm from first BO row, ending with a WS row. Count sts and place a marker in the center of the row.

Shape right side
Row 1 [RS]: Work to 2 sts before marker, k2tog, turn.
Rows 2-7: Work even in seed st.
Row 8 [WS]: Knit. This forms a row of purl bumps on the RS, which you will use when making the strap casing.
Rows 9-15: Work in stockinette beg with a knit row.

To form casing: With a spare needle, pick up the first purl bump on the RS made by Row 8 above. Hold the spare needle behind your LH needle. Insert RH needle into first st on LH needle, then into first st on spare needle and knit these 2 sts together. *Repeat with next purl bump and next st, then slip first st on RH needle over second to BO 1 st. Repeat from * until all sts are bound off.

Shape left side
Row 1 [RS]: Join yarn to second half of sts with RS facing, ssk, work to end.
Work Rows 2-15 and casing as for right side.

UPPER BACK
Join yarn to 73 [83, 93, 101, 111] held sts with RS facing.
Row 1: BO 2 [2, 3, 3, 3] sts, work to marker, turn.
Row 2 [WS]: BO 2 [2, 3, 3, 3] sts, work to end.
Row 3: Ssk, work to last 2 sts, k2tog. 2 sts dec'd.

Row 4: P1, work in seed st to last st, p1.
Rep Rows 3-4 4 [4, 6, 6, 8] times more. 59 [69, 73, 81, 87] sts. Work even, if necessary, until back measures 1.5 [1.75, 2, 2.25, 2.5]"/3.5 [4.5, 4.5, 5.5, 6]cm from first BO row, ending with a RS row. Knit 1 WS row, then work 7 rows stockinette beg with a knit row. Form casing as for fronts.

STRAPS (make 1)
With dpn, CO 3 sts. Work i-cord for 45 [50, 55, 60, 60]"/115 [125, 140, 150, 150]cm. K3tog and fasten off.

FINISHING

Weave in ends and block to finished measurements, gently stretching out the i-cord strap while it is wet. The 4x1 Broken Rib has a tendency to bias, which should be countered with blocking.

Use safety pin to thread strap through casings, beg and end at center front. Try on and adjust straps.

ABOUT CHERYL NIAMATH

Cheryl Niamath lives and knits in Vancouver, Canada. Her very first design, Fetching fingerless gloves, was a surprising success. Her designs have appeard in Knitty, knitscene, Interweave Knits and other collections. Find her online at www.fetchingknits.thruhere.net or on Ravelry as CherylN.

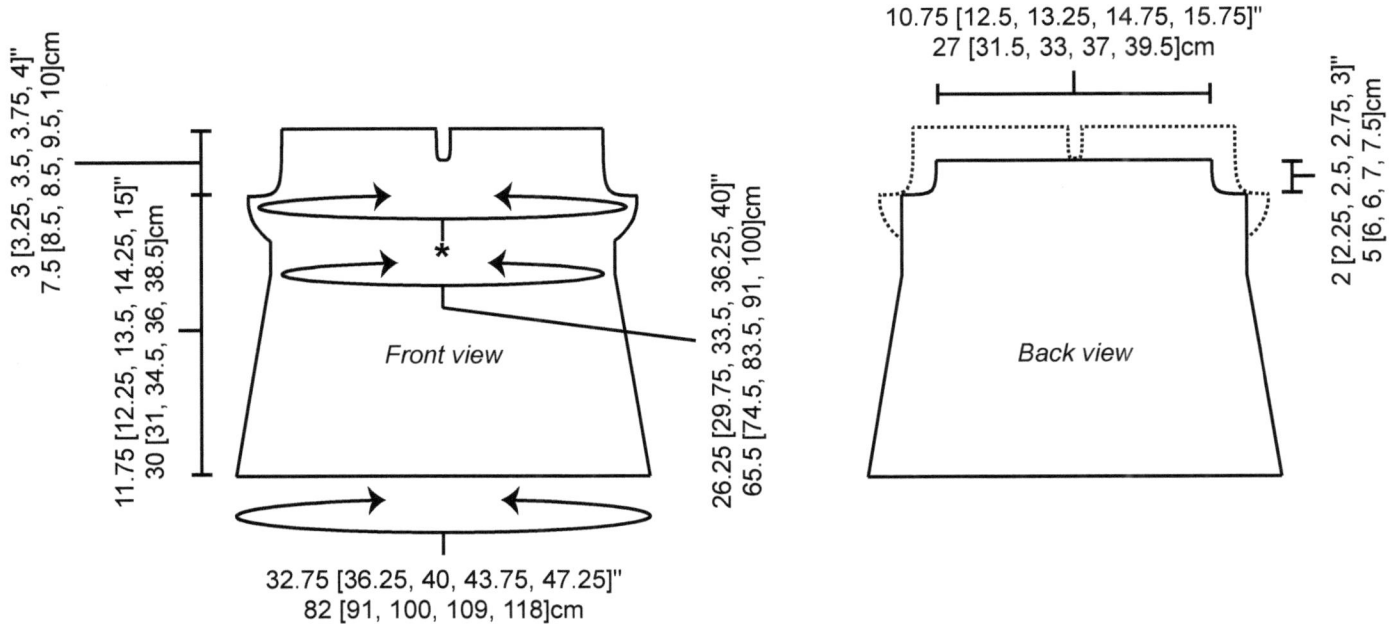

*see table at beginning of pattern for full bust circumferences

BEACH VINES PULLOVER
BY GWEN KERN

INTERMEDIATE

Inspired by the salt-loving vines of the beach morning glory, this casual sweater combines the easy fit of beachwear with an elegant vine lace design on the sleeve. The result is a feminine but comfortable top layer, perfect for warding off the evening chill during long walks on the sand.

SIZE
XS [S, M, L, 1X, 2X, 3X]
Shown in size S

FINISHED MEASUREMENTS
Chest: 32 [35.75, 40, 43.75, 48, 52.25, 56]"/80 [89.5, 100, 109.5, 120, 130.5, 140]cm
Length: 22.25 [22.75, 23.25, 23.75, 24.75, 25.75, 27.25]"/56.5 [58, 59.5, 60.5, 63, 65.5, 69.5]cm

MATERIALS
Blue Sky Alpacas Skinny Dyed Cotton [100% cotton; 150yd/137m per 50g skein]; color: Pear; 6 [6, 7, 8, 8, 9, 10] skeins

24"/60cm US #6/4mm circular needle
29"/74cm US #8/5mm straight needles

4 stitch markers
Tapestry needle

GAUGE
19 sts/24 rows = 4"/10cm in stockinette with larger needles

STITCH INSTRUCTIONS
RLI (right lifted increase): Use the right needle to pick up the stitch below the next stitch on the left needle. Place it on the left needle, then knit into it. 1 st inc'd.

LLI (left lifted increase): Use the left needle to pick up the back of the stitch 2 below stitch just knitted, then knit into it. 1 st inc'd.

Vine Lace (panel of 18 sts):
Row 1 [RS]: [K1, yo, k2, ssk, k2tog, k2, yo] twice.
Rows 2 and 4 [WS]: Purl.
Row 3: [Yo, k2, ssk, k2tog, k2, yo, k1] twice.
Rep Rows 1-4.

PATTERN NOTES
This sweater is knitted top-down in pieces, in order to allow for lacy raglan increases while providing side and sleeve seams to add stability to the loosely knit fabric. Each piece starts at the neck edge and is knitted downward.

PATTERN
BACK AND FRONT (make 2 alike)
With larger needles, cast on 40 [47, 53, 56, 60, 60, 63] sts. Purl 1 row.

Raglan Increase Row [RS]: K2, yo, k to last 2 sts, yo, k2. 2 sts inc'd.
Next Row [WS]: Purl.
Rep these 2 rows 18 [19, 21, 24, 27, 32, 35] more times. 78 [87, 97, 106, 116, 126, 135] sts. Work 8 [8, 8, 6, 4, 2, 2] rows even.

Waist dec row [RS]: K2, ssk, k to last 4 sts, k2tog, k2. 2 sts dec'd.
Repeat Waist Dec Row every 6th row 4 more times. 68 [77, 87, 96, 106, 116, 125] sts. Work even in st st until work measures 13 [13.5, 14, 14.5, 15, 16.5, 17.5]"/33 [34.5, 35.5, 37, 38, 42, 44.5]cm from CO edge, ending with a WS row.

Waist inc row [RS]: K2, RLI, k to last 2 sts, LLI, k2. 2 sts inc'd.
Repeat Waist Inc Row every 6th row 4 more times. 78 [87, 97, 106, 116, 126, 135] sts. Work even in st st until work measures 18 [18.5, 19, 19.5, 20.5, 21.5, 23]"/45.5 [47, 48.5, 49.5, 52, 54.5, 58.5]cm from CO edge, ending with a WS row. Change to smaller needles.

Next row [RS]: Knit.
Next row [WS]: P1, knit to last st, p1.
Rep these 2 rows until garter st band measures 1.75"/4.5cm, ending with a RS row. BO all sts kwise.

SLEEVES
With larger needles, CO 26 sts.
Set-up row [WS]: P4, pm, p18, pm, p4.

Raglan inc row [RS]: K2, yo, k to marker, sl m, work Vine Lace Pattern over 18 sts, sl m, k to last 2 sts, yo, k2.
Purl 1 row.
Rep these 2 rows 18 [19, 21, 24, 27, 32, 35] more times. 64 [66, 70, 76, 82, 92, 98] sts. Work 4 rows even.

Sleeve dec row [RS]: K2, ssk, k to marker, sl marker, work Vine Lace Pattern over 18 sts, sl marker, k to last 4 sts, k2tog, k2. 2 sts dec'd.

Rep Sleeve Dec Row every 4th row 0 [0, 2, 8, 16, 25, 26] times, then every 6th row 14 [14, 14, 10, 5, 0, 0] times. 34 [36, 36, 38, 38, 40, 44] sts. Work even in patt until sleeve measures 16.5 [17, 17, 17.5, 17.5, 18, 18.5]"/42 [43, 43, 44.5, 44.5, 45.5, 47]cm from last Raglan Inc Row, removing markers on last row (WS). Change to smaller needles.

Next row [RS]: Knit.
Next row [WS]: P1, knit to last st, p1.
Repeat these 2 rows until garter st band measures 1"/2.5cm, ending with a RS row. BO all sts kwise.

FINISHING
Mattress stitch the side, sleeve and raglan seams.

With smaller needle and beginning at back left corner of neck edge, RS facing, pick up and knit 1 st in each st around neck edge, placing a marker at each seam (4 markers). 124 [138, 150, 156, 164, 164, 170] sts. Join to work in the round.
Purl 1 rnd.
Neck dec rnd: *Ssk, k to 2 sts before marker, k2tog, sl marker, repeat from * to end of round. 8 sts dec'd.
Rep these 2 rnds three more times. 92 [106, 118, 124, 132, 132, 138] sts. BO all sts pwise.

Weave in ends and block.

ABOUT GWEN KERN
Gwen Kern (sticksandstring on Ravelry) is an attorney by profession and a poet by temperament. She loves to design sweaters and often finds inspiration in nature. She lives in, and adores, Pittsburgh.

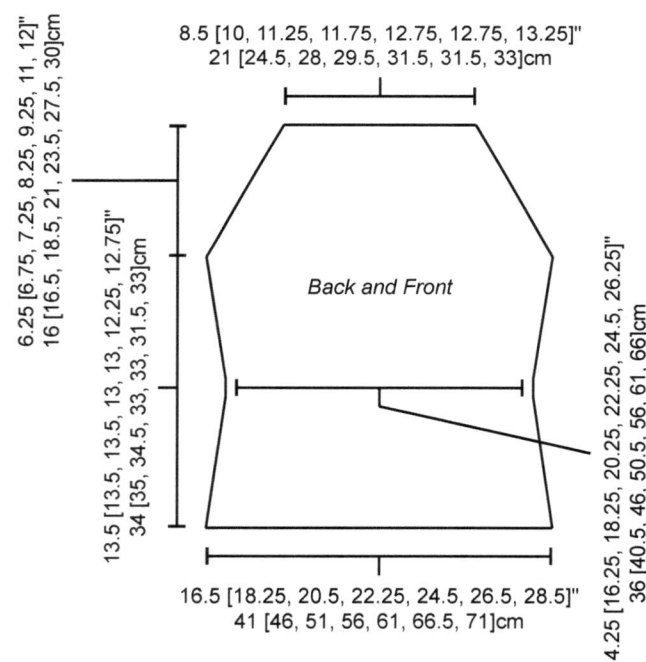

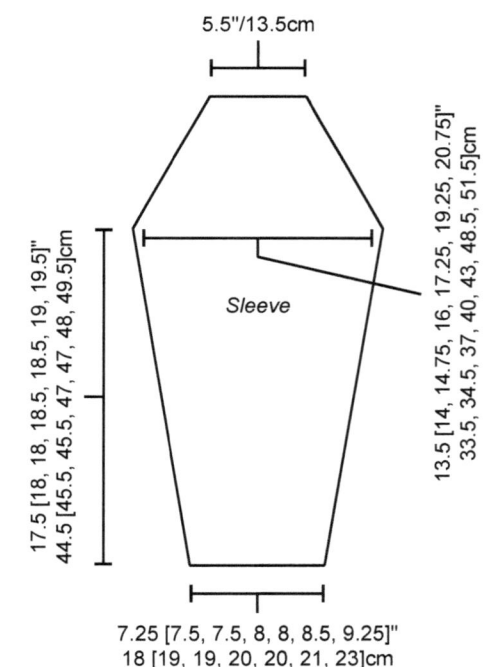

CLASSIC CABLED CREW

BY KAREN BOURQUIN

INTERMEDIATE

This casual cropped crew neck gives a new spin on some of our most favorite stitches and techniques like cables, moss stitch and stockinette stitch. Inspiration came from the desire to create a comfy sweater that one could dress up or down –but always feel at home in.

SIZE
S [M, L, XL]
Shown in size S

FINISHED MEASUREMENTS
Chest: 37 [41.5, 45.5, 49.5]"/92.5 [103, 113.5, 124]cm
Length: 20.5 [21.5, 22.5, 23.5]"/52 [54.5, 57, 59.5]cm

MATERIALS
Berroco Peruvia [100% wool; 174yd/160m per 100g skein]; color #7135 Caliente; 6 [6, 7, 8] skeins

US #8/5mm straight needles
16"/40cm US #6/4mm circular needle

Cable needle
Tapestry needle
Stitch marker

GAUGE
19 sts/28 rows = 4"/10cm over chart patt with larger needles

PATTERN
BACK
With smaller needles, CO 90 [100, 110, 120] sts. Work 4 rows of k1, p1 rib. Change to larger needles. Beg and end as indicated for your size, work following chart until piece measures 19.5 [20.5, 21.5, 22.5]"/49.5 [52, 54.5, 57]cm from CO, ending with a WS row.

Shape right shoulder
Row 1 [RS]: Work 30 [35, 38, 43] sts in patt, turn.
Row 2 [WS]: Work even.
Row 3: Work to last 2 sts, k2tog. 1 st dec'd.
Rep Rows 2-3 two times more. 27 [32, 35, 40] sts.
BO all sts.

Shape left shoulder
Row 1: Join yarn to rem sts with RS facing and BO 30 [30, 34, 34] sts, work in patt to end. 30 [35, 38, 43] sts.
Row 2 [WS]: Work even.
Row 3: Ssk, work to end. 1 st dec'd.
Rep Rows 2-3 two times more. 27 [32, 35, 40] sts.
BO all sts.

FRONT
Work same as Back until piece measures 18 [19, 19.75, 20.75]"/45.5 [48, 50.5, 53]cm from CO, ending with a WS row.

Shape left shoulder
Row 1 [RS]: Work 37 [42, 45, 50] sts in patt, turn.
Row 2 [WS]: BO 2 sts, work to end.
Row 3: Work even.
Rep Rows 2-3 four times more. 27 [32, 35, 40] sts rem.
Work even until piece measures 20.5 [21.5, 22.5, 23.5]"/52 [54.5, 57, 59.5]cm.
BO all sts.

Shape right shoulder
Row 1: Join yarn to rem sts with RS facing and BO 16 [16, 20, 20] sts, work in patt to end. 37 [42, 45, 50] sts.
Row 2 [WS]: Work even.
Row 3: BO 2 sts.
Rep Rows 2-3 four times more. 27 [32, 35, 40] sts.
Work even until piece measures 20.5 [21.5, 22.5, 23.5]"/52 [54.5, 57, 59.5]cm.
BO all sts.

SLEEVES
With smaller needles, CO 48 sts. Work 4 rows of k1, p1 rib. Change to larger needles. Beg at St 3 and ending with St 48 (indicated with

green lines), work following chart for 4 rows.
Inc row [RS]: K1, m1, work in patt to last st, m1, k1. 2 sts inc'd.
Rep Inc Row on every 4th row 4 [8, 12, 20] times more, then every 6th row 14 [12, 10, 5] times. Work the first 2 [3, 3, 3] pairs of inc'd sts into the patt, then work all subsequent inc'd sts in stockinette. 86 [90, 94, 100] sts.
Work even until sleeve measures 17 [17, 18, 18]"/43 [43, 45.5, 45.5] cm from CO.
BO all sts.

FINISHING

Block pieces to measurements. Sew shoulder seams.

Neckband: With circular needle, RS facing and beg at right shoulder seam, pick up and knit 40 [40, 44, 44] sts across back neck, then 50 [50, 56, 56] sts across front neck. 90 [90, 100, 100] sts. Pm and join to work in the round. Work k1, p1 rib for 2.5"/6.5cm. Bind off loosely in rib. Fold band to WS and slip stitch the BO edge in place at the pick-up rnd.

Sew sleeves to body, matching center cable on sleeve to shoulder seam. Sew side and underarm seams. Weave in ends.

ABOUT KAREN BOURQUIN

Karen considers herself fortunate to live on a Pacific Northwest Island where inspiration for designing and neccessity for knitted garments combine to make a perfect knitter's environment. Find her online at http://docksideknits.wordpress.com and as oceangrl on Ravelry.

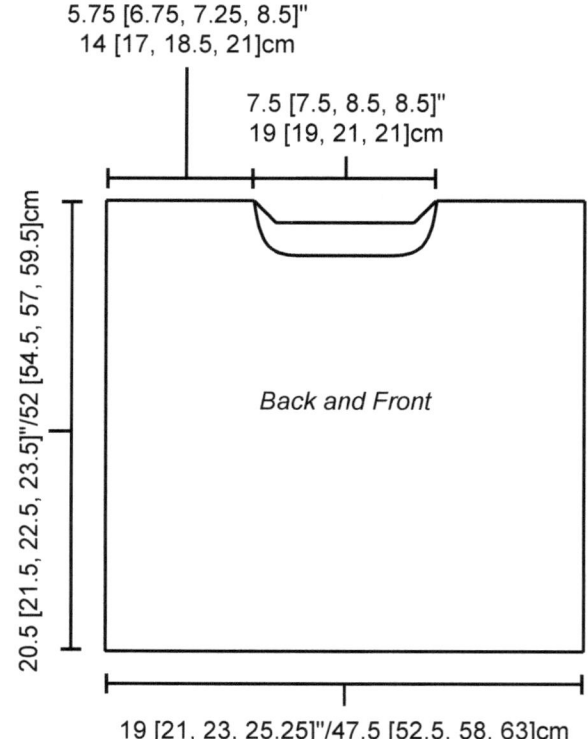

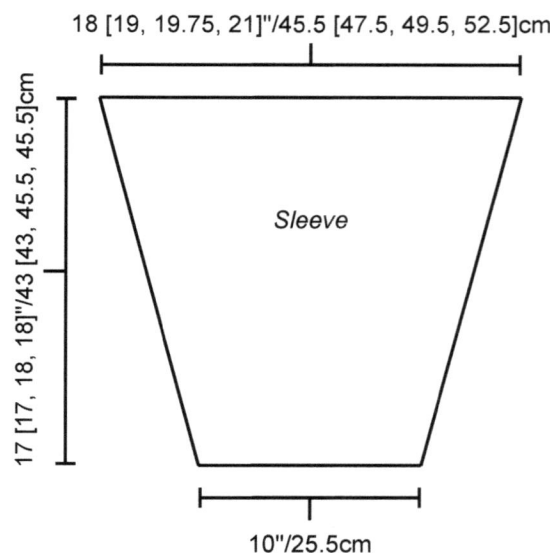

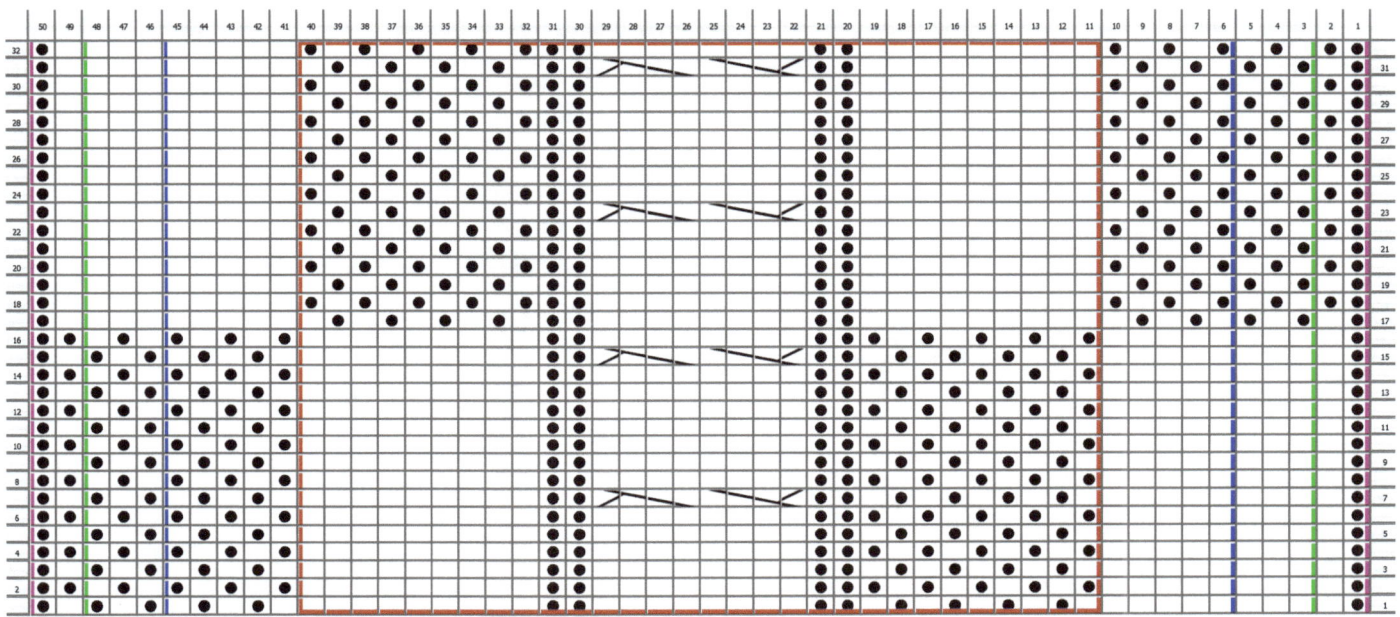

Legend:

- • **purl** — RS: purl stitch / WS: knit stitch
- □ **knit** — RS: knit stitch / WS: purl stitch
- ⧖ **c4 over 4 left** — RS: sl4 to CN, hold in front. k4, k4 from CN / WS: none defined

CHART NOTES

Red box indicates patt repeat (30 sts and 32 rows).
For sizes S and XL, beg at St 11 and end with St 40.
For size M, beg at St 6 and end with St 45 (indicated with blue lines).
For size L, beg at St 1 and end with St 50 (indicated with pink lines).

25

ZIGGY

BY PAMELA WYNNE

EXPERIENCED

Ziggy is a lightweight A-line cardigan with a chevron pattern on the yoke and sleeves. The mosaic stitch pattern is created with slipped stitches, using just one color per row.

SIZE
XS [S, M, L, 1X, 2X, 3X, 4X, 5X]
Shown in size M

FINISHED MEASUREMENTS
Chest: 27.25 [31.25, 35.25, 39.25, 43.25, 47.25, 51.25, 55.25, 59.25]"/68.5 [78.5, 88.5, 98.5, 108, 118, 128, 138, 148]cm
Length: 21 [21.5, 22, 22.5, 23, 23.5, 24, 24.5, 24.5]"/53.5 [55, 56, 57.5, 58.5, 60, 61.5, 62.5, 62.5]cm

MATERIALS
[MC] A Verb for Keeping Warm Metamorphosis [70% merino wool, 30% silk; 385yd/352m per 115g skein]; color: Thai Iced Tea; 2 [2, 2, 2, 3, 3, 3, 3, 4] skeins
[CC] A Verb for Keeping Warm Metamorphosis [70% merino wool, 30% silk; 385yd/352m per 115g skein]; color: Undyed; 1 [2, 2, 2, 2, 2, 2, 2, 3] skeins

24"/60cm US #4/3.5mm circular needle
Two US #3/3.25mm dpns for working i-cord
Two US #2/3mm dpns for working i-cord

Six or seven 5/8"/16mm buttons
Stitch marker
Tapestry needle
Safety pins

GAUGE
24 sts/34 rows = 4"/10cm in stockinette stitch with largest needles
27 sts/42 rows = 4"/10cm in mosaic patt with largest needles

PATTERN NOTES
Mosaic Pattern
The zig-zag pattern used in this sweater is a slip stitch, or mosaic pattern. Each row is worked using only one color; the colorwork effect is created by slipping stitches from the previous row.

How to read the chart: The column to the right of the chart indicates which color to use for each row. Any stitches shown as the opposite color (the color that you're not working with for that row) are slipped stitches. To slip a stitch, hold the working yarn to the wrong side of the fabric, and slip the stitch purlwise, without twisting it, from the left needle to the right. Carry your yarn loosely behind the slipped stitches.

When working chart, the column to the right of the chart also indicates the direction in which to work each row. You will alternate between the CC and MC, working two right-side rows (one with each color, following the chart from right to left), followed by two wrong-side rows (one with each color, following the chart from left to right). You must use a circular needle, so that you can slide your stitches back and forth.

Maintain the zig-zag pattern as you shape the armholes, neck, and shoulders. When binding off one or two stitches, carry the opposite color over those stitches loosely; the carried yarn will be hidden inside a seam or i-cord edging. When binding off three or more stitches, break off the yarn and start a new ball as needed.

If you'd like an extra-stable and clean edge for seaming, do not slip the first or last stitch of any row when working chart pattern. Instead, work the first and last stitches of each row in stockinette stitch.

Attached I-cord
Using a provisional cast-on and double-pointed needles, cast on 4 sts. Do not turn. *Slide the stitches to the right end of the needle. Bring the working yarn behind the cast-on stitches and knit the first stitch, pulling the working yarn snug. Continue to knit until there is 1 stitch remaining on the LH needle. Slip this st pwise. Dip the needle into the edge of your knitting and pick up a stitch. Pass the slipped stitch over the picked-up stitch. Repeat from *.

You may not find yourself attaching the i-cord to every single edge stitch – instead, just gently tug the i-cord stitches into place, then dip into the edge stitch closest to your needle.

Attached I-cord Buttonhole
Work three rows of i-cord without attaching it to the edge (instead of slipping and passing the last stitch, knit it, then slide stitches back to the right for the next row). Skip two edge-stitch rows, then resume working attached i-cord.

PATTERN
BACK
Using MC and circular needle, loosely cast on 96 [108, 120, 132, 144, 156, 168, 180, 192] sts. Work in stockinette. Dec 1 st at each end of every 18th row twice, then every 19th row 4 times. 84 [96, 108, 120, 132, 144, 156, 168, 180] sts. Work even until piece measures 13.5"/34.5cm, ending with a WS row.

Shape armholes
BO 3 [5, 6, 8, 9, 11, 12, 14, 15] sts at beg of next 2 rows. Dec 1 st at each end of every RS row 3 [4, 6, 7, 9, 10, 12, 13, 15] times. 72 [78, 84, 90, 96, 102, 108, 114, 120] sts. Work 1 WS row even.

Join CC and begin working chart. Continue until piece measures 20.5 [21, 21.5, 22, 22.5, 23, 23.5, 24, 24]"/52 [53.5, 54.5, 56, 57, 58.5, 60, 61, 61]cm from CO, ending with Row 4, 8, or 12 of chart.

Shape neck and shoulders
Row 1 [RS] [CC]: BO 5 [6, 6, 7, 7, 8, 8, 9, 10] sts, work to end of row in patt.

Right shoulder:
Row 2 [RS] [MC]: K11 [11, 13, 13, 15, 15, 16, 17, 19] sts. Pm and turn. Complete right shoulder shaping on only these 11 [11, 13, 13, 15, 16, 17, 19] sts.
Row 3 [WS] [CC]: Work in patt to end.
Row 4 [WS] [MC]: P2tog, work 4 [4, 5, 5, 6, 6, 6, 7, 8] sts in patt, BO 5 [5, 6, 6, 7, 7, 8, 8, 9] sts. Break yarn, set aside chart, and complete final 2 rows of shoulder in stockinette.
Row 5 [RS] [MC]: Knit.
Row 6 [WS] [MC]: BO rem 5 [5, 6, 6, 7, 7, 7, 8, 9] sts.

Left shoulder:
Row 2 [RS] [MC]: Join yarn, BO 40 [44, 46, 50, 52, 56, 60, 62, 62] sts for back neck. Work to last 5 [6, 6, 7, 7, 8, 8, 9, 10] sts in patt. BO 5 [6, 6, 7, 7, 8, 8, 9, 10] sts. 11 [11, 13, 13, 15, 16, 17, 19] sts.
Row 3 [WS] [CC]: Work in patt to end.
Row 4 [WS] [MC]: BO 5 [5, 6, 6, 7, 7, 8, 8, 9] sts, work 4 [4, 5, 5, 6, 6, 6, 7, 8] sts in patt, p2tog. Set aside chart and complete final 2 rows of shoulder in stockinette.
Row 5 [RS] [MC]: Knit.
Row 6 [WS] [MC]: BO rem 5 [5, 6, 6, 7, 7, 7, 8, 9] sts.

FRONTS (make 2)
Using MC and circular needle, loosely CO 48 [54, 60, 66, 72, 78, 84, 90, 96] sts.
Dec 1 st on outside edge on every 18th row twice, then every 19th row 4 times. 42 [48, 54, 60, 66, 72, 78, 84, 90] sts. Work even until piece measures 13.5"/34.5cm, ending with a WS row for Left Front/RS row for Right Front.

Shape armhole
BO 3 [5, 6, 8, 9, 11, 12, 14, 15] sts at beg of next row.
Dec 1 st at beg of row for Left Front/end of row for Right Front, every RS row 3 [4, 6, 7, 9, 10, 12, 13, 15] times. 36 [39, 42, 45, 48, 51, 54, 57, 60] sts. Work 1 WS row even.

Join CC and begin working chart. Continue until piece measures 17.75 [18, 18.25, 18.5, 19.75, 19, 19.25, 19.5, 19.5]"/45 [45.5, 46.5, 47, 50, 48.5, 49, 49.5, 49.5]cm from CO, ending with a RS row for Left Front/WS row for Right Front.

Shape neck
BO 11 [12, 11,12, 12, 14, 15, 14, 13] sts at beg of next row.
BO 2 sts at neck edge on every other row 2 [2, 3, 3, 3, 3, 4, 4, 4] times.
Dec 1 st at neck edge every other row 6 [7, 7, 8, 9, 9, 8, 10, 11] times. 15 [16, 18, 19, 21, 22, 23, 25, 28] sts.

Work even until piece measures measures 20.5 [21, 21.5, 22, 22.5, 23, 23.5, 24, 24]"/52 [53.5, 54.5, 56, 57, 58.5, 60, 61, 61]cm from CO, ending with Row 4, 8, or 12 of chart to match back piece. Follow appropriate shoulder shaping directions for the Left or Right shoulder below.

Left shoulder
Row 1 [RS] [CC]: BO 5 [6, 6, 7, 7, 8, 8, 9, 10] sts, work in patt to end.
Row 2 [RS] [MC]: Work even in patt.
Row 3 [WS] [CC]: Work even in patt.
Row 4 [WS] [MC]: Work 6 [6, 7, 7, 8, 8, 8, 9, 10] sts in patt, BO 5 [5, 6, 6, 7, 7, 8, 8, 9] sts. Set aside chart and complete final 2 rows of shoulder in stockinette.
Row 5 [RS] [MC]: Knit.
Row 6 [WS] [MC]: BO rem 5 [5, 6, 6, 7, 7, 8, 8, 9] sts.

Right shoulder
Row 1 [RS] [CC]: Work 10 [10, 12, 12, 14, 14, 15, 16, 18] sts in patt, BO 5 [6, 6, 7, 7, 8, 8, 9, 10] sts.
Row 2 [RS] [MC]: Work even in patt.

Row 3 [WS] [CC]: Work even in patt.
Row 4 [WS] [MC]: BO 5 [5, 6, 6, 7, 7, 8, 9] sts, work in patt to end. Set aside chart and complete final 2 rows of shoulder in stockinette.
Row 5 [RS] [MC]: Knit.
Row 6 [WS] [MC]: BO rem 5 [5, 6, 6, 7, 7, 8, 8, 9] sts.

SLEEVES (make 2)
Sleeves are worked flat from the top down.

With MC and circular needle, CO 14 [16, 16, 18, 18, 20, 20, 22, 22] sts. Begin working chart, starting with Row 1, St 6 (5, 5, 1, 1, 6, 6, 5, 5). As you increase sts at the edges of the piece, incorporate the new sts into the mosaic patt.

Shape cap
Next row: Use backward loop method to CO 3 sts, work in patt to end.
Rep last row 3 more times. 26 [28, 28, 30, 30, 32, 32, 34, 34] sts.

Inc 1 st at each end of every 2nd row 23 [11, 11, 10, 12, 12, 12, 11, 12] times, then every 4th row 0 [1, 2, 4, 4, 5, 6, 8, 6] times, then every 2nd row 0 [11, 12, 11, 12, 12, 13, 12, 15] times. 72 [74, 78, 80, 86, 90, 94, 96, 100] sts.

Use backward loop method to CO 3 [5, 6, 8, 9, 11, 12, 14, 15] sts at beg of next 2 rows. 78 [84, 90, 96, 104, 112, 118, 124, 130] sts.

Shape sleeve
Dec 1 st at beg and end of every 10th row 5 [0, 0, 0, 0, 0, 0, 0] times, then every 8th row 8 [14, 11, 9, 0, 0, 0, 0] times, then every 6th row 0 [0, 4, 7, 19, 14, 12, 11, 9] times, then every 4th row 0 [0, 0, 0, 0, 7, 10, 12, 15] times. 52 [56, 60, 64, 66, 70, 74, 78, 82] sts. Work even until sleeve measures 11.5"/29.5cm from underarm. BO.

FINISHING

Weave in all ends on wrong side. Block all pieces to measurements. Sew shoulder seams. Sew sleeves into armholes. Using mattress stitch, sew side and underarm seams.

With safety pins, mark buttonhole locations along right front edge. Space the buttonholes evenly, with the top buttonhole 3 sts below the top neck edge.

With larger dpn, beginning at left front neck edge, work attached i-cord edging around neck edge. When you reach the end of the right front neck, work 1 row of i-cord without attaching it to the edge (this will make a nice turn at the corner), then continue to work attached i-cord along buttonhole edge, working buttonholes when you come to the places you've marked. Continue around bottom hem and up button edge to provisional cast-on, working one row of unattached i-cord at each corner. When you reach the left front neck edge, break yarn, leaving a 12-inch tail. Unzip provisional cast-on and graft ends of i-cord together.

With smaller dpn, work attached i-cord around bottom edge of sleeve. Unzip the provisional cast-on and graft ends of i-cord together as above.

Sew buttons opposite buttonholes.
Weave in ends and steam block i-cord edging as needed.

ABOUT PAMELA WYNNE
Pamela Wynne is a knitting designer, historian, and all-around rabble-rouser. She lives and works with her dog The Crushinator in Flint, Michigan and at flintknits.com.

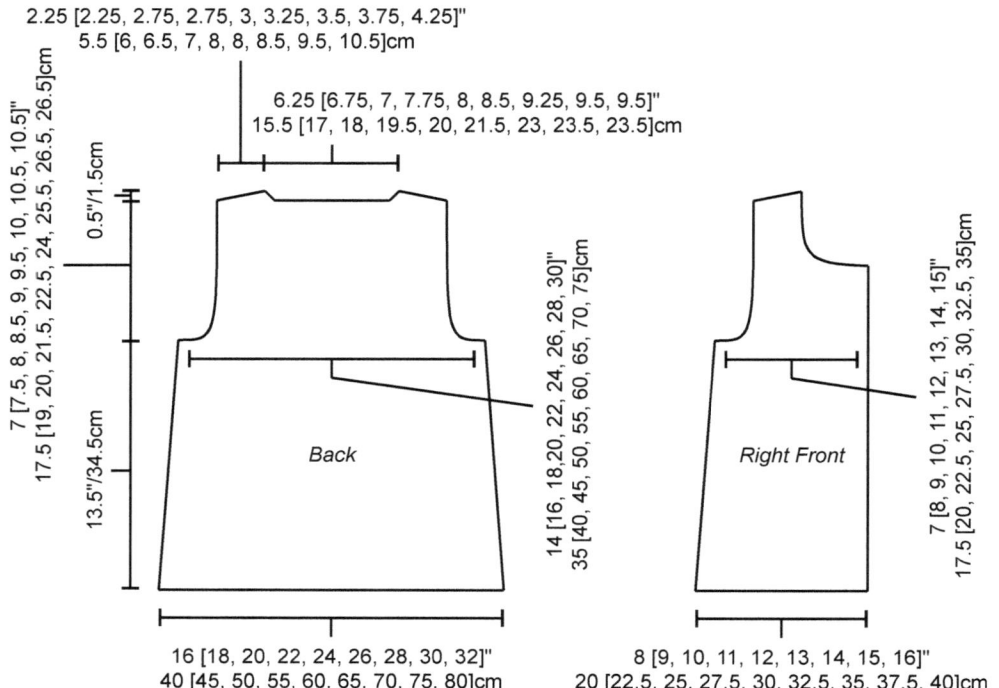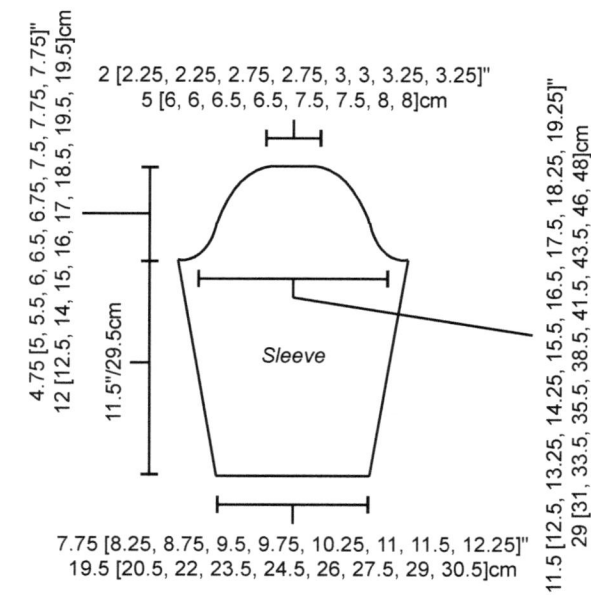

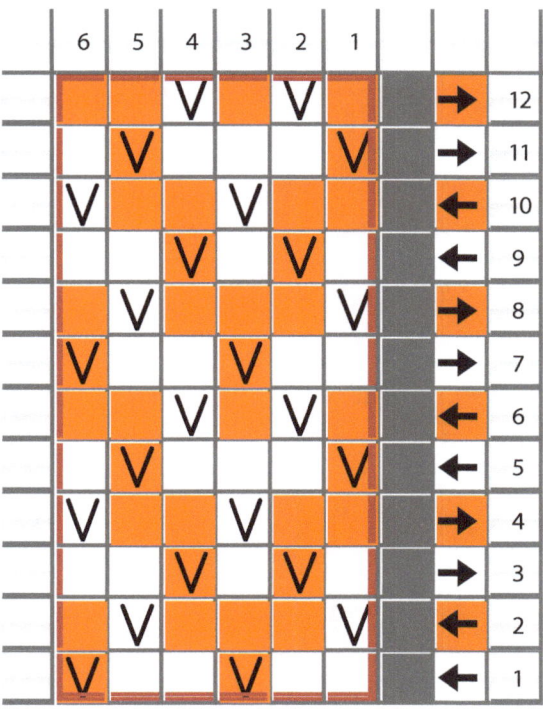

Legend:

	arrow L
←	Work chart from right to left

	No Stitch
■	RS: Placeholder - No stitch made.

	knit
□	RS: knit stitch WS: purl stitch

	slip
V	RS: Slip stitch as if to purl, holding yarn in back WS: Slip stitch as if to purl, holding yarn in front

	arrow R
→	Work chart from left to right

KNOTS AND CABLES VEST
BY ROSALYN JUNG

EXPERIENCED

This crossover vest in a tweedy felted wool is highly textured with braided cables and purl knots that resemble bird tracks in the sand, dandelion flurries flying through the air or wildflowers in bloom across a meadow. A shawl collar, bold button, and rib cap sleeves finish it off in cozy comfort.

Why choose this yarn? It suits the casual, outdoorsy feel of the stitch patterns. More importantly, felted wool has minimal elasticity which helps the horizontal upper bodice hold its shape without sagging due to the weight of the skirt.

SIZE
S [M, L, 1X]
Shown in size M

FINISHED MEASUREMENTS
Chest (closed, with 5"/12.5cm front overlap): 34 [38, 43, 48]"/87 [97, 110, 123]cm
Length: 27.25 [28.75, 30.25, 32]"/70 [72.5, 77, 81]cm

MATERIALS
Rowan Felted Tweed Aran [50% wool, 25% alpaca, 25% viscose; 95yd/87m per 50g skein]; color 720 Pebble; 8 [10, 12, 14] skeins

24" or 29"/60cm or 74cm US #8/5mm circular needle
24" or 29"/60cm or 74cm US #6/4mm circular needle
Two US #6/4mm double pointed needles for i-cord

1.5"/38mm decorative button
Cable needle
Stitch markers
Tapestry needle

GAUGE
16 sts/22 rows = 4"/10cm in Knot Stitch with larger needles

STITCH INSTRUCTIONS
W&t (wrap and turn)
If next st is knit: Sl next st pwise wyib, bring yarn to front between needles, return slipped st to LH needle, turn work.
If next st is purl: Sl next st pwise wyif, bring yarn to back between needles, return slipped st to LH needle, turn work.

I-cord
With dpn, CO 3 sts. Knit 1 row. *Do not turn work. Draw yarn firmly across back of work and knit row again. Rep from * to desired length.

PATTERN NOTES
This garment is knit flat in pieces. The skirt is knit first, then the right front ribbed band is picked up and knit along its edge, followed by the waistband. Back and fronts are knit sideways, from underarm seam to underarm seam, and sewn to the waistband.

PATTERN
SKIRT
With larger circular needle, CO 153 [174, 195, 216] sts.
Patt set-up row [RS]: P3, pm, work Knot St over 9 [12, 15, 18] sts, pm, work Cable chart over 13 sts, pm, work Knot St over 9 [12, 15, 18] sts, pm, work Right Side chart over 22 [25, 28, 31] sts, pm, work Cable chart over 13 sts, pm, work Knot St over 9 [12, 15, 18] sts, pm, work Cable chart over 13 sts, pm, work Left Side chart over 22 [25, 28, 31] sts, pm, work Knot St over 9 [12, 15, 18] sts, pm, work Cable chart over 13 sts, pm, work Knot St over 9 [12, 15, 18] sts, pm, k7, pm, k2.
Patt set-up row [WS]: K2, p7, work patts as established to last 3 sts, k3.
Continue as established until skirt measures 12 [13, 13, 14]"/30.5 [33, 33, 35.5]cm, ending with a WS row. 133 [154, 175, 196] sts. Leave sts on needle. Cut yarn.

Ribbed front edge
With smaller circular needle, RS facing and beg at right bottom corner, pick up and knit 48 [54, 54, 60] sts along front edge of skirt.

Row 1: *K3, p3; rep from * to end.
Rep last row eight more times. BO in rib. Do not fasten off last stitch, but leave on needle with yarn attached.

Ribbed waistband
Using smaller circular needle holding last st from ribbed front edge, RS facing, pick up and knit 5 sts from top of ribbed front edging (6 sts on needle), then purl across sts from larger circular needle, decreasing 0 [4, 5, 6] sts evenly spaced. 139 [156, 176, 196] sts.
Next row [WS]: P1 [0, 2, 4], *k3, p3; rep from * to end.
Next row [RS]: *K3, p3; rep from * to last 1 [0, 2, 4] sts, knit to end.
Rep last 2 rows 5 more times. Knit 1 WS row.
BO all sts.

UPPER BACK
Worked from left side seam to right side seam.
With larger needle, CO 7 sts.
Row 1 [WS]: Purl.
Row 2 [RS]: CO 6 [6, 7, 7] sts. Knit.
Rows 3-6: Rep Rows 1-2 twice. 25 [25, 28, 28] sts.
Row 7 [WS] [armhole CO row]: Pm, use cable method to CO 13 sts, pm, CO 19 [19, 22, 25] sts. Purl. 57 [57, 63, 66] sts.
Row 8: K1, work Knot St to marker, work Cable chart over 13 sts, work Knot St to last st, k1.
Row 9: P1, work patts as established to last st, p1.
Work as established by last 2 rows until back measures 4.5 [5.25, 6, 7]"/11.5 [13.5, 15, 18]cm from armhole CO row, ending with a RS row.
Neck BO row [WS]: BO 3 sts, work to end.
Continue in established patts until back measures 6 [6.5, 7.5, 8]"/15 [16.5, 19, 20.5]cm from neck BO row, ending with a RS row.
Neck CO row [WS]: CO 3 sts, work to end.
Continue in established patts until back measures 4.5 [5.25, 6, 7]"/11.5 [13.5, 15, 18]cm from neck CO row, ending with a RS row.
Armhole BO row [WS]: BO 32 [32, 35, 38] sts, work to end. 25 [25, 29, 29] sts.
Next row [RS]: BO 6 [6, 7, 7] sts, knit to end.
Purl 1 row.
Rep last 2 rows twice more.
BO rem 7 [7, 8, 8] sts.

UPPER RIGHT FRONT
Worked from right side seam to front.
With larger needle, CO 7 sts.
Row 1 [WS]: Purl.
Row 2 [RS]: CO 6 [6, 7, 7] sts. Knit.
Rows 3-6: Rep Rows 1 and 2. 25 [25, 28, 28] sts.
Row 7 [WS] [armhole CO row]: Pm, use cable method to CO 13 sts, pm, CO 19 [19, 22, 25] sts. Purl. 57 [57, 63, 66] sts.
Row 8: K1, work Knot St to marker, work Cable chart over 13 sts, work Knot St to last st, k1.
Row 9: P1, work patts as established to last st, p1.
Work as established by last 2 rows until piece measures 4.5 [5.25, 6, 7]"/11.5 [13.5, 15, 18]cm from armhole CO row, ending with a RS row.

Shape neck
BO 4 sts at beg of every WS row 12 [9, 12, 12] times. BO 3 sts at beg of every WS row 3 [7, 5, 6] times.

UPPER LEFT FRONT
Worked from left side seam to front.
With larger needle, CO 7 sts.
Row 1 [RS]: Knit.
Row 2 [WS]: CO 6 [6, 7, 7] sts. Purl.
Rows 3-6: Rep Rows 1 and 2. 25 [25, 28, 28] sts.
Row 7 [RS] [armhole CO row]: Pm, use cable method to CO 13 sts, pm, CO 19 [19, 22, 25] sts. K1, work Knot St to marker, work Cable Chart over 13 sts, work Knot St to last st, k1. 57 [57, 63, 66] sts.
Row 8: P1, work patts as established to last st, p1.
Work as established until piece measures 4.5 [5.25, 6, 7]"/11.5 [13.5, 15, 18]cm from armhole CO row, ending with a WS row.

Shape neck
BO 4 sts at beg of every RS row 12 [9, 12, 12] times. BO 3 sts at beg of every RS row 3 [7, 5, 6] times.

FINISHING
Block pieces to schematic measurements using the pin-and-spritz method. Seam shoulders.

Inside Ties
With dpns, work 2 i-cord ties, each 12" long, attaching 1 tie to inside right side seam and the other tie to end of inside waistband rib.

Collar
With WS facing and smaller needle, pick up and knit 1 st in every st up left front neck edge, 3 sts in every 4 rows across back neck, and 1 st in every st down right front neck edge. Count sts and adjust to a multiple of 6 + 3 in the first row.
Rows 1 and 2: *K3, p3; rep from * to last 3 sts, w&t.
Rows 3-20: Work in established rib patt to 3 sts before last wrapped st, w&t.
Rows 21-22: Work to end, picking up and working wraps tog with wrapped sts.
Loosely BO all sts.

Sleeve edging
With RS facing and smaller needle, pick up and knit 3 sts in every 4 rows around armhole. Count sts and adjust to a multiple of 6 + 2 in the first row.
Row 1 [WS]: P1, *k3, p3; rep from * to last st, p1.
Row 2 [RS]: K1, *k3, p3; rep from * to last st, k1.
Rep Rows 1-2 three times more. BO loosely in rib.

Sew side seams. Sew upper bodice to waistband.

Button loop and button
With dpn, pick up and knit 3 sts from right front waistband edge. Work i-cord for 1.5"/4cm, or as needed to fit your button. Fasten off, and use yarn tail to sew end of cord in place. Use yarn to sew large outside button in place on left front waistband, making a shank under the button, and adjusting placement as necessary. (Garment was designed with a 5"/12.5cm overlap, but you may prefer more or less.)
Weave in ends.

ABOUT ROSALYN JUNG

Rosalyn is delightfully immersed in a second career teaching and designing in her life-long passions: knitting and sewing. She is college trained in fashion design and that technical background shines through in her teaching and designing. Aside from her creative pursuits she makes time for family and friends, travel and ballroom dance.

KNOT STITCH

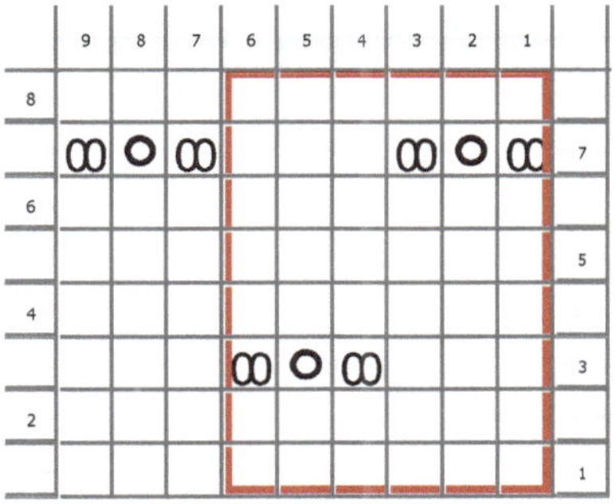

CABLE

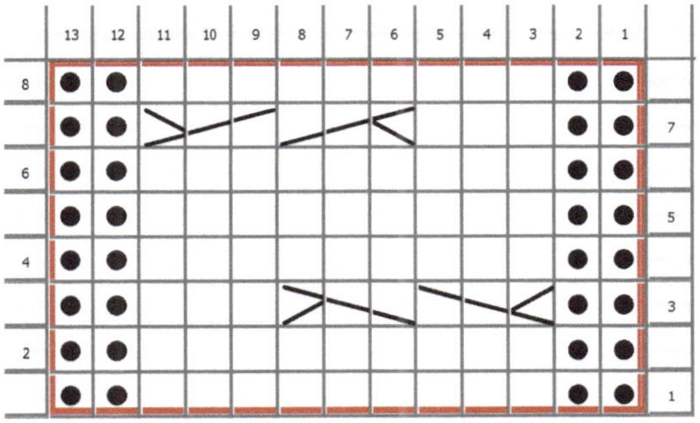

CHART NOTES

For Right Side chart, beg at St 1 for all sizes and work to line for your size: green [purple, yellow, blue]. For Left Side chart, beg at line for your size (green [purple, yellow, blue]) and work to last st. For both Side Charts, work Rows 1-8 5 [6, 6, 7] times, then Rows 9-28 once, then repeat Rows 29-32 to end.

Knot St chart is shown as a multiple of 6 sts + 3. If directed to work Knot St over a number of sts that is multiple of 6, work the sts within the red pattern repeat box only.

35

Legend:

⊙	**purl** RS: purl stitch WS: knit stitch
☐	**knit** RS: knit stitch WS: purl stitch
⤢⤢	**c3 over 3 left** RS: sl3 to CN, hold in front. k3, k3 from CN WS: none defined
∞ O ∞	**knot** RS: P3tog and leave sts on left needle, yo, purl the same 3 sts tog again. WS:
⤢⤢	**c3 over 3 right** RS: sl3 to CN, hold in back. k3, then k3 from CN WS: none defined
⤢	**c2 over 2 left** RS: sl 2 to CN, hold in front. k2, k2 from CN WS: none defined
⤢	**c3 over 2 left** RS: sl3 to CN, hold in front. k2, then k3 from CN WS: none defined
╱	**k2tog** RS: Knit two stitches together as one stitch WS: Purl 2 stitches together
■	**No Stitch** RS: Placeholder - No stitch made. WS: none defined
╲	**ssk** RS: Slip one stitch as if to knit, Slip another stitch as if to knit. Insert left-hand needle into front of these 2 stitches and knit them together WS: Purl two stitches together in back loops, inserting needle from the left, behind and into the backs of the 2nd & 1st stitches in that order
⤢	**c3 over 2 right** RS: sl2 to CN, hold in back. k3, then k2 from CN WS: none defined
⤢	**c2 over 2 right** RS: sl2 to CN, hold in back. k2, k2 from CN WS: none defined

RIGHT SIDE

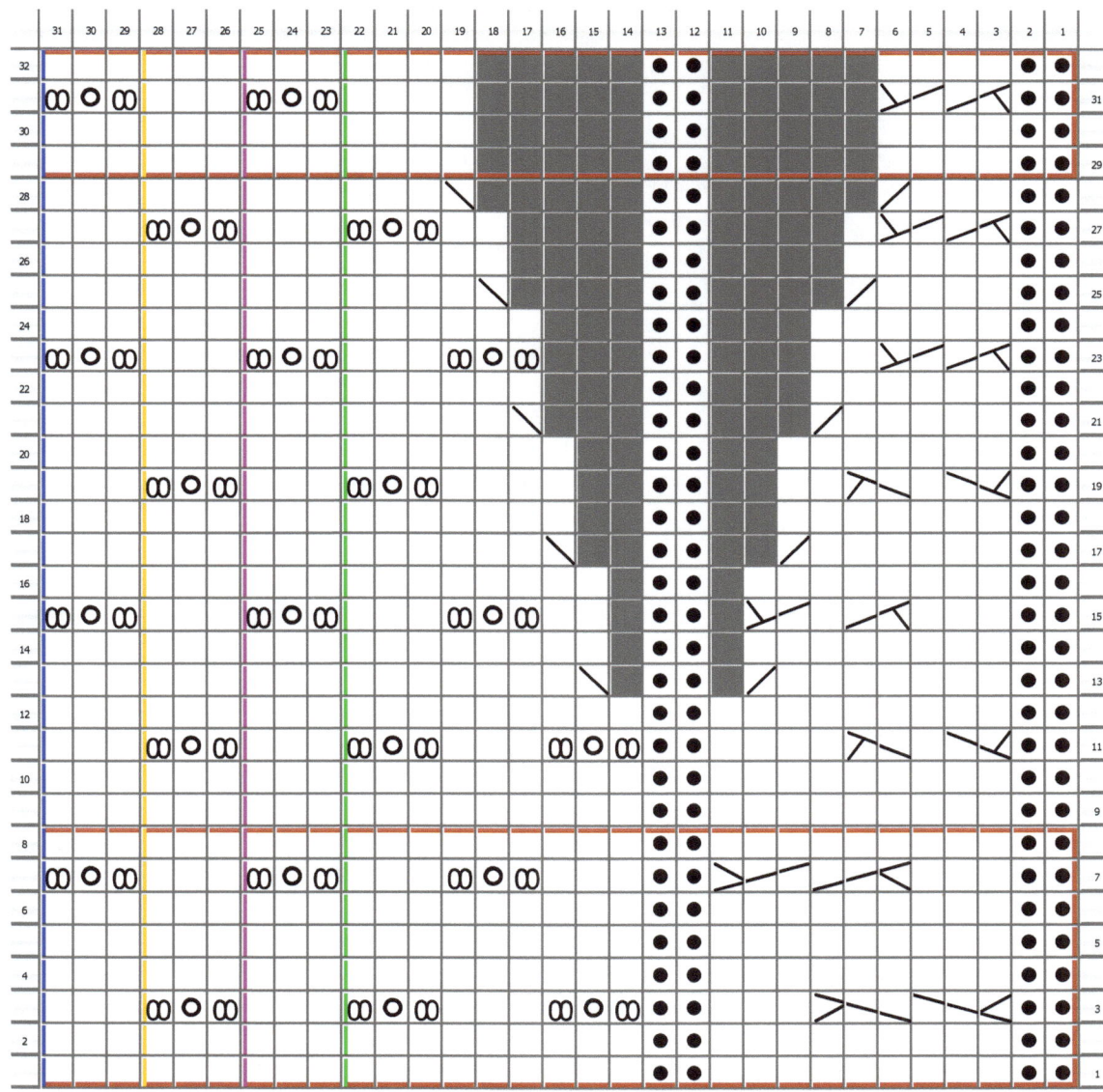

37

LEFT SIDE

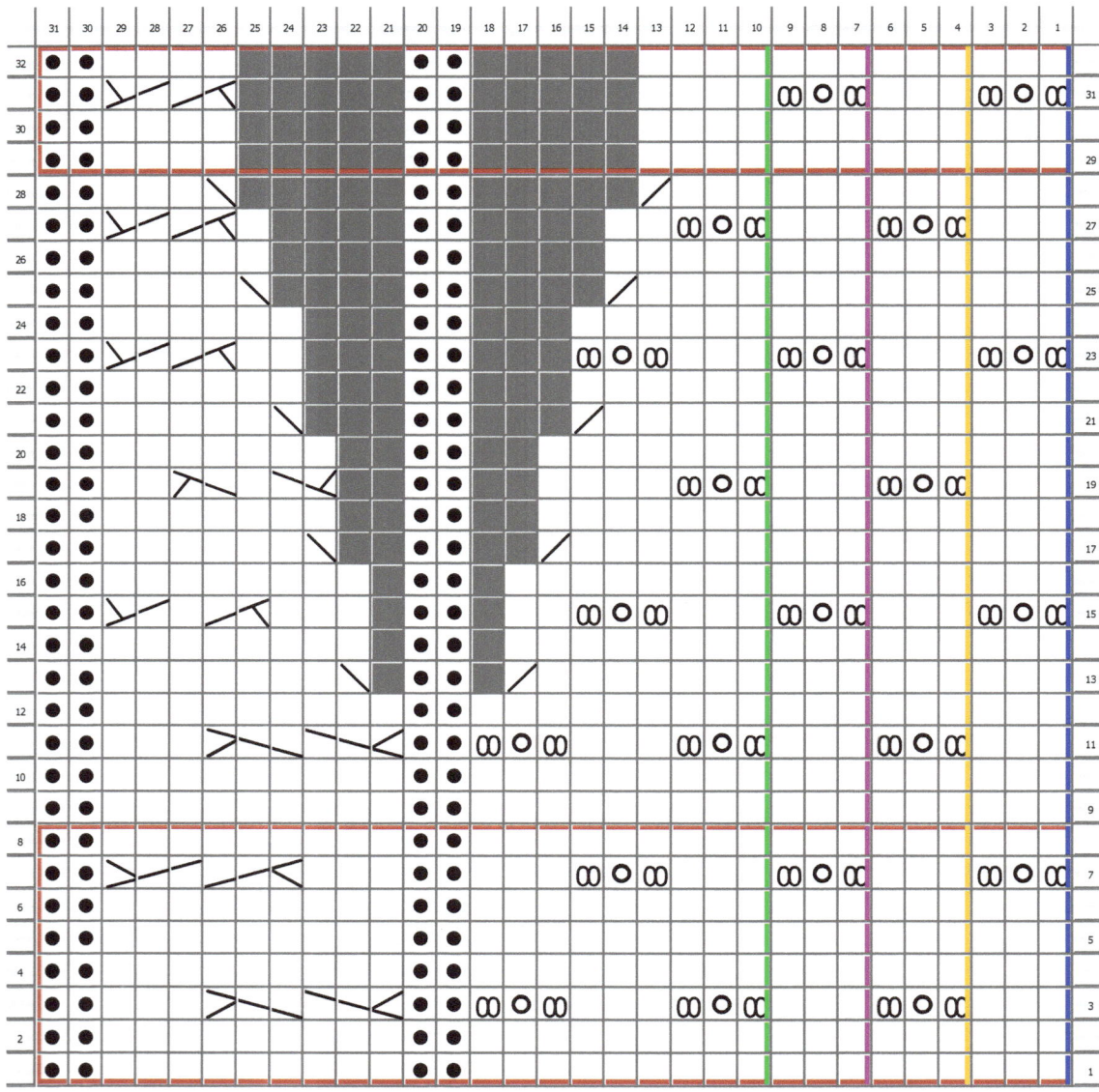

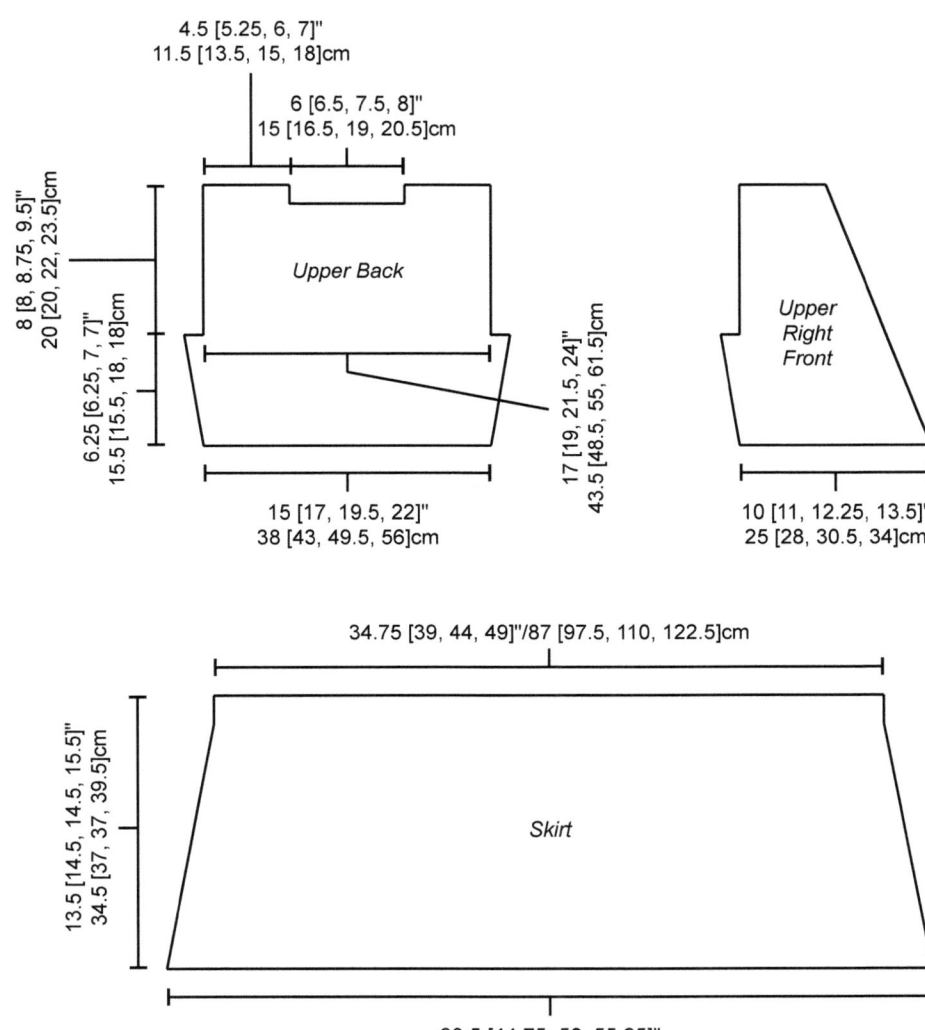

SOPHIA GOES TO HOUDAN

BY SYLVIA CANNIZZARO

INTERMEDIATE

This classic short jacket knit in DK-weight yarn at a firm gauge incorporates a twisted stitch pattern worked on both right and wrong sides, with stitches picked up to knit up the body and sleeves. Close with clasps or a zipper.

SIZE
XS [S, M, L, 1X, 2X]
Shown in size S

FINISHED MEASUREMENTS
Chest: 32 [36, 40, 44, 48, 52]"/81.5 [91.5, 101.5, 112, 123, 132]cm
Length: 20.25 [21, 22, 24, 24.75, 25.75]"/51.5 [53, 56, 61.5, 63, 65.5]cm

MATERIALS
The Sanguine Gryphon Free Range [100% organic wool; 285yd/260m per 113g skein]; color: Houdan; 5 [5, 6, 7, 8, 8] skeins.

US #3/3.25mm straight needles
US #2/2.75mm straight needles

US C/3.25mm crochet hook
Cable needle
Stitch holder
Tapestry needle
5-7 clasps

GAUGE
24 sts/32 rows = 4"/10cm in stockinette with smaller needles
24 sts of Waistband and Cuff Chart = 3.25"/8cm wide, blocked, with larger needles

PATTERN NOTES
When working the cuffs, bands, and collar, note that all the crossed knit RS/purl WS stitches are worked through the back loop. These crosses can be worked with a cable needle, as indicated, but it is much faster to work them without the needle. There are excellent instructions for this available online (and in the Fall 2010 Interweave Knits, accompanying a pattern by Meg Swansen).

PATTERN
BACK WAISTBAND
With larger needles, CO 24 sts. Work Row 1 of Waistband and Cuff Chart [RS], then rep Rows 2-5 until band measures 16 [18, 20, 22, 24, 26]"/40.5 [45.5, 51, 56, 61, 66]cm. Work Row 6. BO. Wash and block.

FRONT WAISTBAND (make 2)
With larger needles, CO 24 sts. Work Row 1 of Waistband and Cuff Chart [RS], then rep Rows 2-5 until band measures 8 [9, 10, 11, 12, 13]"/20.5 [23, 25.5, 28, 30.5, 33]cm. Work Row 6. BO. Wash and block.

CUFF (make 2)
With larger needles, CO 24 sts. Work Row 1 of Waistband and Cuff Chart [RS], then rep Rows 2-5 until cuff measures 8 [9, 10, 10, 10.5, 11]"/20 [23, 25.5, 25.5, 26.5, 28]cm. Work Row 6. BO. Wash and block.

BACK
With smaller needles, RS facing, pick up and knit 98 [110, 122, 134, 146, 158] sts along back waistband.
Row 1 [WS]: Purl tbl.
Work even in stockinette until piece measures 11.5 [11.5, 12, 13.5, 14, 14.5]"/29 [29, 30.5, 34.5, 35.5, 37]cm from bottom edge of band, ending with a WS row.

Shape armholes
BO 5 [6, 6, 6, 7, 7] sts at beg of next two rows. BO 4 sts at beg of next two rows. Dec 1 st at each end on every RS row 2 [4, 6, 6, 8, 11] times. 76 [82, 90, 102, 108, 114] sts.
Work even until armholes measure 8 [8.75, 9.25, 9.75, 10, 10.5]"/20.5 [22, 23.5, 25, 25.5, 26.5]cm, ending with a WS row.

Shape shoulders
BO 7 [8, 9, 11, 11, 11] sts at beg of next two rows. BO 6 [7, 8, 10, 11, 11]

sts at beg of next two rows. BO 6 [7, 8, 9, 10, 11] sts at beg of next two rows. Place rem 38 [38, 40, 42, 44, 48] sts on holder for back neck.

LEFT FRONT
With smaller needles, RS facing, pick up and knit 49 [55, 61, 67, 73, 79] sts along front waistband.
Row 1 [WS]: Purl tbl.
Work even in stockinette until piece measures 11.5 [11.5, 12, 13.5, 14, 14.5]"/29 [29, 30.5, 34.5, 35.5, 37]cm from bottom edge of band, ending with a WS row.

Shape armhole
BO 5 [6, 6, 6, 7, 7] sts at beg of next row [RS]. Work 1 row even. BO 4 sts at beg of next row. Dec 1 st at beg of every RS row 2 [4, 6, 6, 8, 11] times. 38 [41, 45, 51, 54, 57] sts.
Work even until armhole measures 6.25 [7, 7.25, 7.75, 8, 8.25]"/16 [18, 18.5, 19.5, 20.5, 21]cm, ending with a RS row.

Shape neck
BO 10 [10, 10, 11, 12, 13] sts at beg of next row [WS]. Work 1 row even. BO 3 sts at beg of next WS row. BO 2 sts at beg of next 2 WS rows. Dec 1 st at end of every RS row 2 [2, 3, 3, 3, 4] times. 19 [22, 25, 30, 32, 33] sts. Work even until armhole measures 8 [8.75, 9.25, 9.75, 10, 10.5]"/20.5 [22, 23.5, 25, 25.5, 26.5]cm, ending with a WS row.

Shape shoulder
BO 7 [8, 9, 11, 11, 11] sts at beg of next row [RS]. Work 1 row even. BO 6 [7, 8, 10, 11, 11] sts at beg of next row. Work 1 row even. BO rem 6 [7, 8, 9, 10, 11] sts.

RIGHT FRONT
With smaller needles, RS facing, pick up and knit 49 [55, 61, 67, 73, 79] sts along front waistband.
Row 1 [WS]: Purl tbl.
Work even in stockinette until piece measures 11.5 [11.5, 12, 13.5, 14, 14.5]"/29 [29, 30.5, 34.5, 35.5, 37]cm from bottom edge of band, ending with a WS row.

Shape armhole
BO 5 [6, 6, 6, 7, 7] sts at beg of next row [WS]. Work 1 row even. BO 4 sts at beg of next row. Dec 1 st at end of every RS row 2 [4, 6, 6, 8, 11] times. 38 [41, 45, 51, 54, 57] sts.
Work even until armhole measures 6.25 [7, 7.25, 7.75, 8, 8.25]"/16 [18, 18.5, 19.5, 20.5, 21]cm, ending with a WS row.

Shape neck
BO 10 [10, 10, 11, 12, 13] sts at beg of next row [RS]. Work 1 row even. BO 3 sts at beg of next RS row. BO 2 sts at beg of next 2 RS rows. Dec 1 st at beg of every RS row 2 [2, 3, 3, 3, 4] times. 19 [22, 25, 30, 32, 33] sts. Work even until armhole measures 8 [8.75, 9.25, 9.75, 10, 10.5]"/20.5 [22, 23.5, 25, 25.5, 26.5]cm, ending with a RS row.

Shape shoulder
BO 7 [8, 9, 11, 11, 11] sts at beg of next row [WS]. Work 1 row even. BO 6 [7, 8, 10, 11, 11] sts at beg of next row. Work 1 row even. BO rem 6 [7, 8, 9, 10, 11] sts.

SLEEVE
With smaller needles, RS facing, pick up and knit 52 [58, 64, 64, 66, 68] sts along cuff.
Row 1 [WS]: Purl tbl.
Work 4 rows even in stockinette.
Inc 1 st at each end of next row [RS], then every 4th row 3 [6, 3, 15, 15, 21] more times, then every 6th row 14 [12, 14, 6, 7, 2] times. 88 [96, 100, 108, 112, 116] sts. Work even until sleeve measures 17 [17, 17.5, 17.5, 18, 18]"/43 [43, 44.5, 44.5, 45.5, 45.5]cm from bottom of cuff, ending with a WS row.

Shape cap
BO 5 [6, 6, 6, 7, 7] sts at beg of next two rows. BO 4 sts at beg of next two rows. Dec 1 st at each end of every RS row 14 [17, 19, 17, 18, 20] times. 42 [42, 42, 54, 54, 54] sts. BO 2 sts at beg of next 6 [6, 6, 8, 8, 8] rows. BO 3 sts at beg of next 2 [2, 2, 4, 4, 4] rows. BO rem 24 [24, 24, 26, 26, 26] sts.

FINISHING
Wash and block all pieces to schematic measurements.
Sew shoulder seams. Set sleeves into armholes and sew side and underarm seams.

Collar
With RS facing, using larger needles, pick up and knit 86 [86, 94, 102, 110, 110] sts around neck, including 38 [38, 40, 42, 44, 48] back neck sts from holder. Work Rows 1-12 of Collar chart. BO.
Using crochet hook, join yarn to the bottom edge of the collar on the right front. Working on the RS, slip st in every st of the first row of the collar. At the end of the collar, ch 1, turn, and slip st in every st around neckline immediately below collar. Fasten off.

Crocheted front bands and collar edging
Beg at bottom right front corner, RS facing, join yarn and sc in 2 of every 3 sts of the waistband, 1 of every 2 rows up the stockinette portion of the right front, and 2 of every 3 rows along short edge of collar. At top corner, ch 1, turn, and work 1 sl st in every sc back to bottom corner. Ch 1, turn, work 1 sl st in every sl st back up to top corner. Ch 1, work 1 sl st in every bound-off st across top of collar.

Ch 1, sc in 2 of every 3 rows along short edge of collar, 1 of every 2 rows down stockinette portion of left front, and 2 of every 3 sts of the waistband. At bottom corner, ch 1, turn, work 1 sl st in every sc back to top left corner. Ch 1, turn, work 1 sl st in every sl st to bottom left corner. Fasten off.

Weave in ends. Steam block all seams. Line up the left and right fronts and determine placement for the clasps. Center one clasp in the waistband, place one just below the collar, and place the remaining clasps evenly spaced between them. Center the hook and eyes over the front bands and using a long piece of wool and a tapestry needle, baste the clasps in place. One at a time, remove the basting wool and sew the clasps in place.

If you prefer a jacket that closes completely, use a zipper instead of the clasps.

ABOUT SYLVIA CANNIZZARO

Sylvia Cannizzaro lives in the Northeast Kingdom of Vermont, where knitting keeps her warm all winter. She blogs at Sligo's Muse. http://sligosmuse.blogspot.com

COLLAR CHART

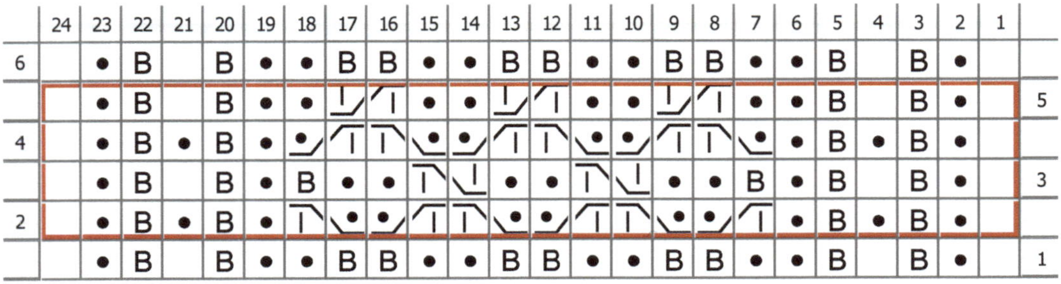

WAISTBAND AND CUFF

	24	23	22	21	20	19	18	17	16	15	14	13	12	11	10	9	8	7	6	5	4	3	2	1	
6	•	B		B	•	•	B	B	•	•	B	B	•	•	B	B	•	•	B		•	B		•	
		•	B		B	•	•	⌐⌐	•	•	⌐⌐		•	•	⌐⌐		•	•	B		•	B		•	5
4		•	B	•	B	•	•	⌐⌐	•	•	⌐⌐		•	•	⌐⌐		•	•	B	•	B		•		
		•	B		B	•	B	•	•	⌐⌐	•	•	⌐⌐	•	•	B	•	B		•	B		•		3
2		•	B	•	B	⌐⌐	•	•	⌐⌐	•	•	⌐⌐	•	•	⌐⌐	•	B	•	B		•	B		•	
		•	B		B	•	•	B	B	•	•	B	B	•	•	B	B	•	•	B		•	B	•	1

Legend:

□ **knit**
RS: knit stitch
WS: purl stitch

• **purl**
RS: purl
WS: knit

B **knit tbl**
RS: Knit stitch through back loop
WS: Purl stitch through back loop

c1 twisted knit over 1 purl Right
RS:
WS: sl1 to cn, hold cn to front, p1 tbl, k1 from cn

c1 twisted knit over 1 purl Left
RS:
WS: sl1 to cn, hold cn to front, k1, p1 tbl from cn

c1 twisted knit over 1 twisted knit Left
RS: sl1 to cn, hold cn to front, k1 tbl, k1 tbl from cn
WS:

c1 twisted knit over 1 twisted knit Right
RS: sl1 to cn, hold cn to back, k1 tbl, k1 tbl from cn
WS:

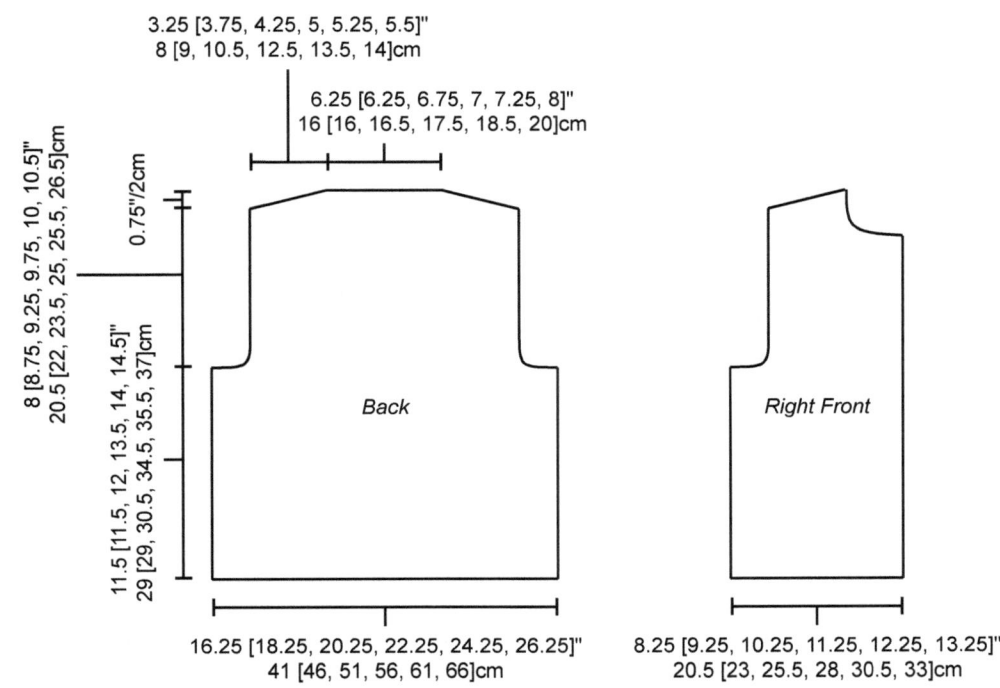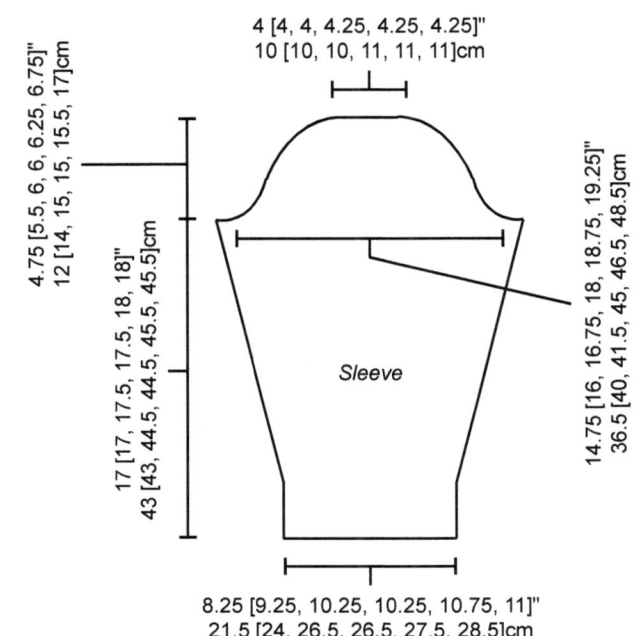

EVERYTHING NICE HOODIE

BY TORI GURBISZ

INTERMEDIATE

The Everything Nice Hoodie is a combination of all the things I love in a sweater - pockets, extra long cuffs with optional thumbholes and an easy fit with varying ribbed side panels give it some shape. Upgrade your weekend wardrobe with this comfy, yet stylish hoodie!

SIZE
XS [S, M, L, 1X, 2X, 3X]
Shown in size M

FINISHED MEASUREMENTS
Chest: 31.5 [34.5, 37.5, 40.5, 42.5, 46.5, 50.5]"/79 [86.5, 94, 101.5, 106.5, 116.5, 126.5]cm
Length: 24.5 [24.75, 25.5, 26.25, 26.5, 27.25, 28]"/61.5 [62.5, 64.5, 66, 67, 69, 70.5]cm

MATERIALS
Three Irish Girls Lindon Merino [100% merino wool; 180 yd/165m per 115g skein]; color: O'Donnell; 6 [7, 7, 7, 8, 8, 9] skeins

32"/80cm US #8/5mm circular needle
47"/120cm US #7/4.5mm circular needle (or two 32"/80cm needles)
Set of US #8/5mm dpn
Set of US #7/4.5mm dpn

Waste yarn or stitch holders
Stitch markers
Yarn needle
Five or six 1"/25mm buttons

GAUGE
16 sts/22 rows = 4"/10cm in stockinette stitch with US 8/5mm needles or size needed to obtain gauge.

STITCH INSTRUCTIONS
3-Needle Bind Off: Have each set of sts on its own needle. Hold needles together with wrong sides of work facing each other. Insert RH needle into first st on front needle, then into first st on back needle and knit the two sts together. *Insert RH needle into next st on front needle, then into next st on back needle and knit the two sts together. Pass first st over second to BO 1 st. Rep from * until all sts are bound off.

PATTERN NOTES
This sweater is knit in one piece from the bottom up. Once the body and sleeves are complete, stitches for the hood are picked up from the neck. The button band is picked up and worked in one piece after the hood is made.

PATTERN
BODY
With smaller circular needle CO 122 [134, 146, 158, 164, 180, 196] sts.

Ribbing set-up row [WS]:
XS: P1, [k1, p1] across next 16 sts, pm, k1, p3, k1, p1, k1, p2, k2, p1, pm (side seam), p1, k2, [p1, k1] twice, p3, k1, pm, [p1, k1] across next 40 sts, p1, pm, k1, p3, k1, p1, k1, p2, k2, p1, pm (side seam), p1, k2, [p1, k1] twice, p3, k1, pm, [p1, k1] to end of row.

S: P1, [k1, p1] across next 18 sts, pm, k1, p3, [k1, p1] across next 6 sts, k2, p1, pm (side seam), p1, k2, p2, [k1, p1] twice, k1, p3, k1, pm [p1, k1] across next 42 sts, p1, pm, k1, p3, [k1, p1] across next 6 sts, k2, p1, pm (side seam), p1, k2, p2, [k1, p1] twice, k1, p3, k1, pm, [p1, k1] to end of row.

M: [K1, p1] across next 22 sts, pm, k1, p3, [k1, p1] across next 6 sts, k2, p1, pm (side seam), p1, k2, p2, [k1, p1] twice, k1, p3, k1, pm, [p1, k1] across next 48 sts, p1, pm, k1, p3, [k1, p1] across next 6 sts, k2, p1, pm (side seam), p1, k2, p2, [k1, p1] twice, k1, p3, k1, pm, [p1, k1] to last st, p1.

L: P1, [k1, p1] across next 22 sts, pm, k1, p3, [k1, p1] across next 6 sts, k2, p2, k1, pm (side seam), k1, p2, k2, p2, [k1, p1] twice, k1, p3, k1, pm, [p1, k1] across next 50 sts, p1, pm, k1, p3, [k1, p1] across next 6 sts, k2, p2, k1, pm (side seam), k1, p2, k2, p2, [k1, p1] twice, k1, p3, k1, pm, [p1, k1] to end of row.

XL: [K1, p1] across next 24 sts, pm, k1, p3, [k1, p1] across the next 6 sts, k2, p2, k1, pm (side seam), k1, p2, k2, p2, [k1, p1] twice, k1, p3, k1, pm, [p1, k1] across next 54 sts, p1, pm, k1, p3, [k1, p1] across next 6 sts, k2, p2, k1, pm (side seam), k1, p2, k2, p2, [k1, p1] twice, k1, p3, k1, pm, [p1, k1] to last st, p1.

2X: P1, [k1, p1] across next 24 sts, pm, k1, p3, [k1, p1] across next 6 sts, k1, p2, k2, p2, k1, pm (side seam), k1, p2, k2, [p1, k1] across next 8 sts, p3, k1, pm, [p1, k1] across next 58 sts, p1, pm, k1, p3, [k1, p1] across next 6 sts, k1, p2, k2, p2, k1, pm (side seam), k1, p2, k2, [p1, k1] across next 8 sts, p3, k1, pm, [p1, k1] to end of row.

3X: P1, [k1, p1] across next 26 sts, pm, k1, p3, [k1, p1] across next 6 sts, k1, [p2, k2] twice, p1, pm (side seam), p1, k2, p2, k2, [p1, k1] across next 8 sts, p3, k1, pm, [p1, k1] across next 62 sts, p1, pm, k1, p3, [k1, p1] across next 6 sts, k1, [p2, k2] twice, p1, pm (side seam), p1, k2, p2, k2, [p1, k1] across next 8 sts, p3, k1, pm, [p1, k1] to end of row.

All sizes: Continue in established rib patt, working sts as they appear (k the knits and p the purls), for 2.5 [2.5, 2.5, 3, 3, 3.5, 3.5]"/6.5 [6.5, 6.5, 7.5, 7.5, 9, 9]cm ending with a WS row.

Right pocket
Note: The fronts of the pockets are knit and then placed on hold. Stitches are picked up from behind the pocket fronts and the body is worked until even with the pockets, then the body and pocket stitches are worked together.

Change to larger circular needle and k18 [18, 21, 22, 23, 26, 28] sts, sl m, work 7 [9, 6, 7, 6, 5, 3] sts in rib patt. Leave rem body sts on smaller circular needle. Turn work and work even in est patt (k the knits and p the purls) over the pocket sts for 8 rows, ending with a RS row.
Shape opening:
Row 1 [WS]: BO 3 [4, 4, 4, 4, 5, 5] sts, work to end.
Row 2 [RS]: Work even.
Row 3: BO 1 [2, 2, 2, 2, 3, 3] sts, work to end.
Row 4: Work to last 3 sts, k2tog, k1. 1 st dec'd.
Row 5: Work even.
Rep Rows 4-5 eight times more.
Work 8 rows even.
Break yarn and place rem 12 [12, 12, 14, 14, 14] sts on waste yarn.

Left pocket

With larger circular needle, RS facing, join yarn at right front edge, pick up and knit 18 [18, 21, 22, 23, 26, 28] from behind right pocket, pm, pick up and knit 7 [9, 6, 7, 6, 5, 3] sts. Work in est rib patt to side seam m, rib to next m, sl m, knit across the back to the next m, sl m, work in rib to the last m slipping the side seam m, k17 [19, 22, 23, 24, 25, 27] sts to end of row.
Next row [WS]: P17 [19, 23, 24, 25, 27], sl sm, work 8 [8, 5, 6, 5, 6, 4] sts in rib, place rem body sts on waste yarn. Turn work and work even in est patt over the pocket sts for 8 rows, ending with a WS row.
Shape opening:
Row 1 [RS]: BO 3 [4, 4, 4, 4, 5, 5] sts, work to end.
Row 2 [WS]: Work even.
Row 3: BO 1 [2, 2, 2, 2, 3, 3] sts, work to end.
Row 4: Work even.
Row 5: Work to last 3 sts, k2tog, k1. 1 st dec'd.
Rep Rows 4-5 eight times more.
Work 8 rows even.
Break yarn and place rem 12 [12, 12, 14, 14, 14] sts on waste yarn.

Place body sts back on circular needle, with RS facing rejoin yarn at lower right edge of left pocket, pick up and knit 8 [8, 5, 6, 5, 6, 4] sts from behind left pocket, pm, pick up and knit 17 [19, 22, 23, 24, 25, 27] sts. Turn work, purl to the first m, work in rib patt to third m (make sure to work est rib patt across newly picked up sts), purl across back to fourth m, work in rib patt to last m, purl to end of row. Continue to work the body even in est patts until it is even with the top edge of the pockets, approx. 7"/18cm from the top of the ribbed band, ending with a WS row.

Join top edge of pockets to main body [RS]: Place live sts from right pocket on a spare needle, hold spare needle in front of body needle and knit corresponding pocket st tog with body st until all of the pocket sts are used up. Work across body to last 12 [12, 12, 14, 14, 14] sts, then repeat for left pocket.

Work even until body measures 16"/40.5cm from CO edge, ending with a WS row. Set body aside on circular needle with yarn attached.

SLEEVES
With smaller DPNs, CO 32 [34, 34, 36, 36, 36, 38] sts, pm and join in the round. Work in k1, p1 rib for 2.75"/7cm.
Make thumbhole:
Right sleeve: Rib 2, with waste yarn work in patt across the next 6 [6, 6, 7, 7, 7, 7] sts, slip these sts back to LH needle, then work them again in main yarn. Rib to end of rnd.
Left sleeve: Rib to last 8 [8, 8, 9, 9, 9, 9] sts, with waste yarn work in patt across the next 6 [6, 6, 7, 7, 7, 7] sts, slip these sts back to LH needle, then work them again in main yarn. Rib to end of rnd.

Both sleeves: Continue in rib until cuff measures 5.5"/14cm. Change to larger needles and stockinette, work even for 6 [6, 6, 6, 4, 2, 2] rnds.
Inc rnd: K1, m1L, knit to last st, m1R, k1. 2 sts inc'd. Rep Inc Rnd on every 4th rnd 0 [0, 1, 3, 5, 5, 11] more times, then every 6th rnd 0 [0, 2, 4, 4, 11, 7] times, then every 8th rnd 7 [8, 7, 5, 4, 0, 0] times. 48 [52, 56, 62, 64, 70, 76] sts. Work even until sleeve measures 21 [21.5, 21.5, 22, 22, 22.5, 22.5]"/53.5 [54.5, 54.5, 56, 56, 57, 57]cm from CO edge. Next rnd, work to 1 [2, 2, 3, 3, 4, 5] sts before marker and place the next 2 [4, 4, 6, 6, 8, 10] sts on a stitch holder or waste yarn. 46 [48, 52, 56, 58, 62, 66] sts. Break yarn leaving a tail for grafting underarm.

YOKE
Join body and sleeves [RS]: Work in patt across right front of body to 2 [3, 3, 4, 4, 5, 6] sts before side seam m, pm for raglan, p1, pm for raglan and place the next 2 [4, 4, 6, 6, 8, 10] sts on a stitch holder or waste yarn. Work across right sleeve sts, pm for raglan, p1 from body, pm for raglan, work in patt across back sts to 2 [3, 3, 4, 4, 5, 6] sts before side seam m, pm for raglan, p1, pm for raglan and place the next 2 [4, 4, 6, 6, 8, 10] sts on a stitch holder or waste yarn. Work across left sleeve sts, pm for raglan, p1 from body, pm for raglan, work in patt to end of row. 210 [222, 242, 258, 268, 288, 308] sts.
Next row [WS]: Work sts as they appear.
Raglan dec row [RS]: *Work in patt to 2 sts before raglan marker, ssk, sl m, p1, sl m, k2tog; rep from * 3 times more, work in patt to end. 8 sts dec'd.
Rep the last 2 rows 19 [20, 22, 24, 25, 27, 29] more times. 50 [54, 58, 58, 60, 64, 68] sts.

HOOD
Note: The remaining back and sleeve stitches are bound off on the WS and picked up on the next RS row, while live stitches from the fronts are held to create a clean look when the hood is down. The bind-offs provide the neck with some structure and help prevent sagging.
Set-up row 1 [WS]: Removing markers as you come to them, purl to first raglan m, BO next 34 [36, 38, 38, 40, 42, 44] sts pwise to last m, purl to end of row.
Set-up row 2 [RS]: Knit to BO sts, pick up and knit 34 [36, 38, 38, 40, 42, 44] sts, knit to end.
Set-up row 3 [WS]: P25 [27, 29, 29, 30, 32, 34], pm, purl to end.

Shape hood
Inc row [RS]: Knit to 1 st before m, m1R, k1, sl m, k1, m1L, knit to end. 2 sts inc'd.
Rep Inc Row on next RS row, then on every 4th row 6 [5, 4, 4, 3, 2, 0] times. 66 [68, 70, 70, 70, 72, 72] sts. Work even until hood measures 10.5 [10.5, 11, 11, 11, 11.5, 11.5]" from pick-up row, ending with a WS row.
Dec row [RS]: Knit to 3 sts before m, ssk, k1, sl m, k1, k2tog, knit to end. 2 sts dec'd.
Rep Dec Row on every 4th row twice more, then on every 2nd row 3 times. 54 [56, 58, 58, 58, 60, 60].
Fold hood with WS together and join top with a 3-needle BO.

FINISHING
Front band
Note: When picking up the bands along the pocket edges there will be two layers of fabric, the body and the pocket fronts. Pick up stitches through both layers of fabric to close and attach the pocket edge to the body.

With smaller circular needle(s) (one very long needle or two shorter), RS facing, pick up and knit 288 [290, 300, 306, 310, 312, 318] sts along body and hood edge, or approximately 2 sts for every 3 rows. Work in k1, p1 rib for 1.5 [1.5, 1.5, 1.5, 2, 2, 2]"/4 [4, 4, 4, 5, 5, 5]cm. BO loosely in rib.

Pocket openings
With smaller circular needle, RS facing, pick up and knit 23 [25, 25, 25, 25, 27, 27] sts along curved pocket opening. Work k1, p1 rib for 6 rows. BO loosely in rib. Whipstitch or use your preferred seaming method to attach short ends of ribbing and vertical edge of pocket to body.

Thumbholes
Remove waste yarn and place the 11 [11, 11, 13, 13, 13, 13] live sts on two smaller dpns, 6 [6, 6, 7, 7, 7, 7] at the top of the thumb opening and 5 [5, 5, 6, 6, 6, 6] at the bottom of the opening. Join yarn and knit across bottom sts, pick up 2 sts in between the two needles, knit across top sts, then pick up two sts between the needles. Pm and join in the round. Knit 2 rnds and BO loosely.

Graft underarms closed. Weave in ends. Block. Sew buttons on left band, spaced evenly about 3"/7.5cm apart. To make button loops, CO 3 sts using smaller dpn and make a 3"/7.5cm i-cord. Fasten off leaving a long tail for sewing. Attach loops where front band and body meet.

ABOUT TORI GURBISZ
Tori has been creating for as long as she can remember in a wide variety of mediums, including wax, paint and yarn. Her secret aspiration was to be a fashion designer when she grew up and knitting is giving her the opportunity to realize that dream. She blogs at http://lachesisandco.blogspot.com and can be found on Ravelry as lachesis77.

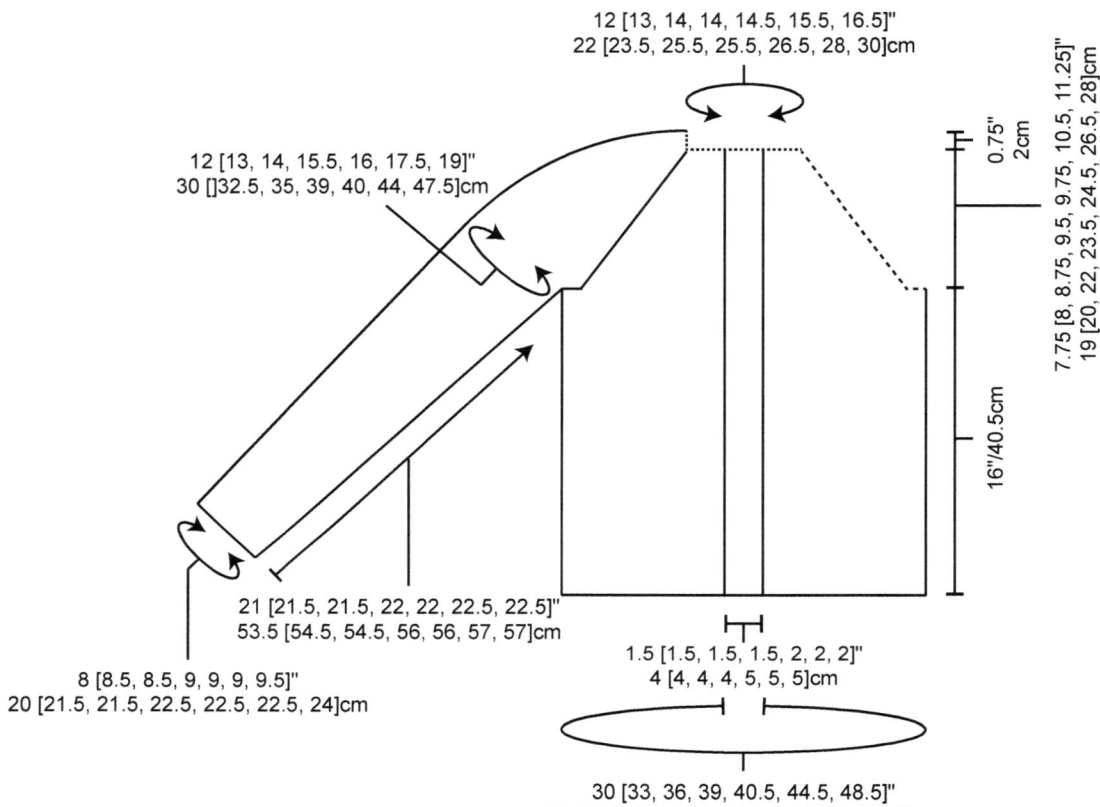

CRESCENT
BY VERA KALTENECKER

EXPERIENCED

Crescent is a top-down sweater with a uniquely constructed saddle or yoke. The body is worked in the round following the outlines of the yoke. The fit is easy to adjust to any woman's body and you'll love the beautiful, flattering sweater once finished.

SIZE
XS [S, M, L, 1X, 2X, 3X]
Shown in size M

FINISHED MEASUREMENTS
Chest: 28.25 [31.25, 34.5, 36.75, 38.25, 40.25, 43]"/71.5 [79.5, 87.5, 93, 97, 103, 109]cm
Length: 22.25 [22.5, 23.25, 23.75, 23.75, 24, 24.25]"/55.5 [56.5, 59, 59.5, 60, 60, 61]cm

Sweater is designed to be worn with negative ease.

MATERIALS
[MC] Yarn Hollow Brocade [60% merino wool, 40% silk; 250yd/228m per 113g skein]; color: Teal; 3 [3, 4, 4, 5, 5, 6] skeins
[CC] Yarn Hollow Brocade; color: Green Jewels; 1 skein

24" or 29"/60cm or 74cm US #6/4mm circular needle
16"/40cm US #6/4mm circular needle
Set of US #6/4mm dpns

Waste yarn
Stitch markers
Tapestry needle
Cable needle

GAUGE
18 sts/24 rows = 4"/10cm in stockinette
21 sts = 4"/10cm wide over bias stockinette

STITCH INSTRUCTIONS
RLI (right lifted increase): Use the right needle to pick up the stitch below the next stitch on the left needle. Place it on the left needle, then knit into it. 1 st inc'd.

LLI (left lifted increase): Use the left needle to pick up the back of the stitch 2 below stitch just knitted, then knit into it. 1 st inc'd.

W&t (wrap and turn)
On a RS row: Sl next st pwise wyib, bring yarn to front between needles, return slipped st to LH needle, turn work.
On a WS row: Sl next st pwise wyif, bring yarn to back between needles, return slipped st to LH needle, turn work.

PATTERN NOTES
This sweater is knit from the top down. The yoke is knit back and forth to the end of the front neck shaping, then joined; then the upper front and back are worked separately to the base of the armholes. At the underarm, back and front are joined together and continued in the round to the hem.

The sleeves are picked up around the armholes and knit down to the cuff, with the cap shaped by short rows.

PATTERN
SET-UP FOR YOKE
With CC and longer circular needle, CO 8 sts.
Rows 1-32: Sl1, knit to end.
After finishing Row 32, do not turn work. Pick up and knit 16 sts along long side of strip, turn work 90 degrees and pick up and knit 8 sts from CO edge of strip. 32 sts.

YOKE
Row 1 [WS]: Sl1, knit to end.
Row 2 [RS]: Sl1, k2, yo, k1, yo, k4, yo, pm, k16, pm, yo, k4, yo, k1, yo, k3. 38 sts.
Row 3: Sl1, knit to end, knitting all yos from previous row tbl.
Row 4: Sl1, k2, yo, k1, yo, knit to m, yo, sl m, work next 16 sts following Chart A, sl m, yo, knit to last 4 sts, yo, k1, yo, k3. 6 sts inc'd.

Row 5: Sl1, knit to marker knitting all yos from previous row tbl, sl m, work next 16 sts following Chart A, sl m, knit to end knitting all yos tbl.
Repeat Rows 4-5 16 [18, 21, 23, 24, 25, 27] times more. 140 [152, 170, 182, 188, 194, 206] sts.
Change to MC. For sizes XS, M, L, 1X, stop working Chart A and knit the 16 sts between the markers on every row until completion of yoke. For sizes S, 2X, 3X, continue working Chart A between the markers.
Rep Rows 4-5 twice more, working sts between markers as directed for your size. 152 [164, 182, 194, 200, 206, 218] sts.

The yoke is now complete and will be closed at center front.
Next row [RS]: Knit to last 2 sts, pm, p2, use backward loop method to CO 8 sts, join to work in the round and p2, pm, k26 [29, 33, 36, 38, 40, 43] sts. 160 [172, 190, 202, 208, 214, 226] sts.

Turn work and resume working back-and-forth to shape armholes.

FRONT TO UNDERARM
Row 1 [WS]: Purl to m, sl m, k12, sl m, p26 [29, 33, 36, 38, 40, 43], turn. 64 [70, 78, 84, 88, 92, 98] sts for front. Place rem unworked sts on waste yarn, leaving the two back markers in place.
Row 2 [RS]: K1, ssk, knit to 1 st before marker, RLI, k1, sl m, work next 12 sts following Chart B, sl m, k1, LLI, knit to last 3 sts, k2tog, k1.
Row 3: Purl to marker, sl m, work next 12 sts following Chart B, sl m, purl to end.
Rep Rows 2-3 four times more. Chart B is complete.
Next row [RS]: K1, ssk, knit to 1 st before marker, RLI, k1, sl m, k12, sl m, k1, LLI, knit to last 3 sts, k2tog, k1.
Next row [WS]: Purl.
Rep last 2 rows 6 [7, 9, 10, 11, 12, 13] times more. Place front sts on waste yarn.

BACK TO UNDERARM
Return to held sts. Leave the first and last 16 [16, 17, 17, 16, 15, 15] sts of the row on hold for the sleeve caps, replace the center 64 [70, 78, 84, 88, 92, 98] sts on needle. Join yarn with RS facing.

Row 1 [RS]: K1, ssk, knit to 1 st before m, RLI, k1, sl m, k16, sl m, k1, LLI, knit to last 3 sts, k2tog, k1.
Row 2 [WS]: Purl.
Rep Rows 1-2 11 [12, 14, 15, 16, 17, 18] times more.

BODY
The remainder of the sweater is worked in the round.
Join back and front [RS]: Over back sts, k1, ssk, knit to 1 st before m, RLI, k1, sl m, k16, sl m, k1, LLI, knit to last 3 sts, k2tog, pm, k1. Use backward loop method to CO 6 [8, 8, 8, 8, 10, 10] sts for underarm.

Put held front sts on a spare needle with RS facing. Work them onto circular needle as foll: K1, pm, ssk, knit to 1 st before m, RLI, k1, sl m, k12, sl m, k1, LLI, knit to last 3 sts, k2tog, pm, k1. Use backward loop method to CO 6 [8 8, 8, 8, 10, 10] sts for underarm. K1 from back. Pm for beg of rnd. 140 [156, 172, 184, 192, 204, 216] sts.

Rnd 1: Knit.
Rnd 2: *Ssk, knit to 1 st before m, RLI, k1, sl m, knit to next m, sl m, k1, LLI, knit to 2 sts before m, k2tog, sl m, knit to next m, sl m; rep from * once more.
Rep Rnds 1-2 until body measures 11"/28cm from underarm or desired length, ending with Rnd 1.

Hem
Rnd 1: Purl.
Rnd 2: Knit.
Rnd 3: *P2tog, purl to m, sl m, purl to m, sl m, purl to 2 sts before m, p2tog, sl m, purl to m, sl m; rep from * once more. 136 [152, 168, 180, 188, 200, 212] sts.
Rnd 4: *Ssk, knit to 1 st before m, RLI, k1, sl m, knit to next m, sl m, k1, LLI, knit to 2 sts before m, k2tog, sl m, knit to next m, sl m; rep from * once more.
Rnd 5: Purl.
Rnd 6: Knit.
Rnd 7: Rep Rnd 3.
Rnd 8: Rep Rnd 4.
BO all sts pwise.

SLEEVE
Place 16 [16, 17, 17, 16, 15, 15] held sleeve cap sts on shorter circular needle. With MC, RS facing, pick up and knit 17 [19, 22, 24, 27, 28, 30] sts from cap sts to underarm, pick up and knit 6 [8, 8, 8, 8, 10, 10] sts from underarm, pick up and knit 17 [19, 22, 24, 27, 28, 30] sts from underarm to cap sts. 56 [62, 69, 73, 78, 81, 85] sts.

Shape cap
Row 1 [RS]: K16 [16, 17, 17, 16, 15, 15], w&t.
Row 2 [WS]: P16 [16, 17, 17, 16, 15, 15], w&t.
Row 3: Knit to last wrapped st, knit wrap tog with st, k1, w&t.
Row 4: Purl to last wrapped st, purl wrap tog with st, p1, w&t.
Rep Rows 3-4 7 [8, 9, 10, 12, 12, 13] times more.
Next rnd: Knit all the way around, picking up and knitting rem wraps tog with their sts. Place a marker at center underarm and treat this as the beg of the rnd from now on.
Work 3 rnds even.
Dec rnd: K2, k2tog, knit to last 4 sts, ssk, k2. 2 sts dec'd.

Rep Dec Rnd on every foll 13th (11th, 7th, 6th, 5th, 4th) rnd 3 [4, 7, 8, 10, 11, 13] more times. 48 [52, 53, 55, 56, 57, 57] sts. Work even until sleeve measures 16"/40.5cm or desired length.

Cuff
Rnd 1: Purl.
Rnd 2: Knit.
Rnd 3: Purl.
Rnd 4: K1, k2tog, knit to last 3 sts, ssk, k1.
Rep Rnds 1-4 once more. 44 [48, 49, 51, 52, 53, 53] sts.
BO purlwise.

FINISHING
Collar
The collar uses short row shaping to raise the front neck slightly, filling in the deep V-opening.
With CC, RS facing, using circular needle and beg in center of back panel, pick up and knit 1 st in each st or row around neck to the center front panel, pick up and knit 12 sts across the center front panel, pick up and knit 1 st in each st or row around neck to the beginning. Pm for beg of rnd. Count sts and adjust to a multiple of 4 on first rnd.
Rnds 1-2: K1, *p2, k2; rep from * to last 3 sts, p2, k1.
Row 3: Work in rib to 12 sts before marker, w&t.
Row 4: Work in rib to 12 sts before marker, w&t.
Rows 5-8: Work in rib to 4 sts before last wrapped st, w&t.
BO in rib, working wraps tog with their sts as you go.

Weave in ends. Block. Enjoy wearing!

ABOUT VERA KALTENECKER
My Ravelry ID is loony, and I've been knitting since my mother showed me how at the age of 5 or 6. I also enjoy spinning, weaving and dyeing but knitting is my first and dearest love, and sometimes I like to share this love by designing knits of all kind.

CHART A

Legend:

▢ **knit**
RS: knit stitch
WS: purl stitch

⦿ **purl**
RS: purl stitch
WS: knit stitch

CHART B

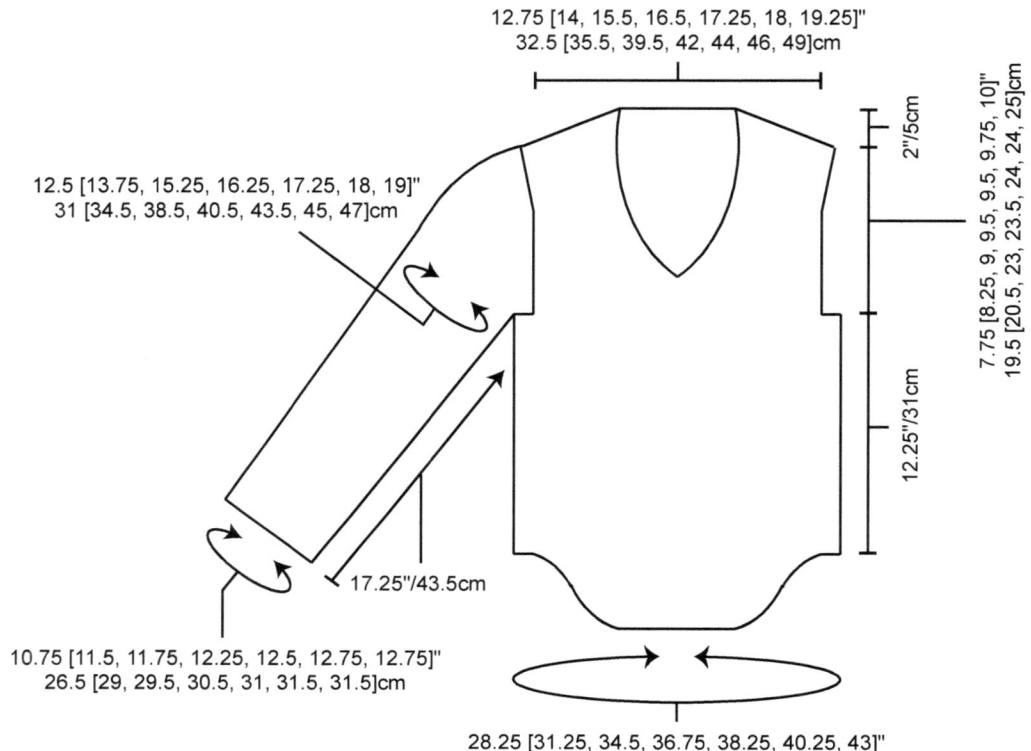

ACKNOWLEDGMENTS

Thank you to the designers who created such beautiful work for the book. Our biggest thanks to photographer Robert Gladys, makeup artist Elle Gemma, and to our models Arabella Proffer, Rachel Harner, Susan Prahst and Terra Incognita, as well as to Abra Forman, whose considerable talents helped bring the project together in its early stages. Sarah Jo Burch helped keep things running so Abra and Shannon could get things done, and MJ Kim did a massive amount of organizational work before we handed everything off to the talented technical editor, Alexandra Virgiel. Elizabeth Green Musselman came late to the team but helped enormously with wrapping up loose ends.

The book wouldn't be nearly as beautiful without the yarns contributed by the companies below.

We'd also like to thank the generous patrons whose Kickstarter support helped make this book series possible.

YARNS FEATURED IN THIS BOOK:

Spirit Trail Fiberworks	(http://www.spirit-trail.net)
Serenknitty	has changed names and is now (http://madcolorfiberarts.com)
Americo Originals	(http://www.americo.ca)
Blue Sky Alpacas	(http://blueskyalpacas.com)
Berroco	(http://www.berroco.com)
A Verb for Keeping Warm	(http://www.averbforkeepingwarm.com)
Rowan	(http://www.knitrowan.com)
The Sanguine Gryphon	has split into two companies since this book was commissioned: (http://verdantgryphon.com) and (http://cephalopodyarns.com)
Three Irish Girls	(http://www.threeirishgirls.com)
Yarn Hollow	(http://www.etsy.com/shop/yarnhollow)

ABOUT COOPERATIVE PRESS

partners in publishing

Cooperative Press (formerly anezka media) was founded in 2007 by Shannon Okey, a voracious reader as well as writer and editor, who had been doing freelance acquisitions work, introducing authors with projects she believed in to editors at various publishers.

Although working with traditional publishers can be very rewarding, there are some books that fly under their radar. They're too avant-garde, or the marketing department doesn't know how to sell them, or they don't think they'll sell 50,000 copies in a year.

5,000 or 50,000. Does the book matter to that 5,000? Then it should be published.

In 2009, Cooperative Press changed its named to reflect the relationships we have developed with authors working on books. We work together to put out the best quality books we can, and share in the proceeds accordingly.

Thank you for supporting independent publishers and authors.

We're on Ravelry as CooperativePress. Please join our low-volume mailing list and check out our other books at...

WWW.COOPERATIVEPRESS.COM

ABOUT FRESH DESIGNS

Shannon Okey wanted to do something to showcase emerging design talent after she left the editorship of a UK print knitting magazine; Fresh Designs is the result. A partnership between talented designers and primarily small/indie yarn companies (all of whom are thanked on the previous page — please help support these remarkable companies when you next shop for yarn), the first 10 Fresh Designs books have also broken the mold for designer compensation. Each time you purchase a Fresh Designs book or pattern, the designers receive a royalty share. We hope you'll enjoy meeting the designers in these pages, and that you'll check out the other books in the Fresh Designs series.

ABBREVIATIONS

alt	alternate
approx	approximately
beg	begin/beginning
BO	bind off
CC	contrasting color
cn	cable needle
CO	cast on
dec	decrease(s)/decreasing
dpn	double pointed needle
est	established
foll	follows/following
inc	increase(s)/increasing
k	knit
k2tog	knit 2 together
kfb	knit into the front and back of the same stitch
kwise	knitwise
LH	left hand
m1	make 1 stitch
M1L	make 1 left
M1R	make 1 right
MC	main color
p	purl
patt	pattern
pm	place marker
p2tog	purl 2 together
psso	pass slipped st over
pwise	purlwise
rem	remain/remaining
rep(s)	repeat(s)
RH	right hand
rnd(s)	round(s)
RS	right side
sl	slip
ssk	slip, slip, knit these 2 sts together
tbl	through the back loop
tog	together
WS	wrong side
wyib	with yarn in back
wyif	with yarn in front
yo	yarn over